Psychology Resources on the World Wide Web

Edward P. Kardas
Southern Arkansas University

Brooks/Cole Publishing Company
I⊕P® An International Thomson Publishing Company

Pacific Grove • Albany • Belmont • Bonn • Boston • Cincinnati
Detroit • Johannesburg • London • Madrid • Melbourne • Mexico City
New York • Paris • Singapore • Tokyo • Toronto • Washington

Acquisitions Editor: *Vicki Knight*
Editorial Assistant: *Stephanie Andersen*
Marketing Team: *Aaron Eden, Lauren Harp, and Margaret Parks*
Production Editor: *Mary Vezilich*
Cover Design & Illustration: *Jennifer Mackres*
Printing and Binding: *Webcom*

For more information, contact:

BROOKS/COLE PUBLISHING COMPANY
511 Forest Lodge Road
Pacific Grove, CA 93950
USA

International Thomson Editores
Seneca 53
Col. Polanco
11560 México, D. F., México

International Thomson Publishing Europe
Berkshire House 168-173
High Holborn
London WC1V 7AA
England

International Thomson Publishing Japan
Hirakawacho Kyowa Building, 3F
2-2-1 Hirakawacho
Chiyoda-ku, Tokyo 102
Japan

Thomas Nelson Australia
102 Dodds Street
South Melbourne, 3205
Victoria, Australia

International Thomson Publishing Asia
60 Albert Street
#15-01 Albert Complex
Singapore 189969

Nelson Canada
1120 Birchmount Road
Scarborough, Ontario
Canada M1K 5G4

International Thomson Publishing GmbH
Königswinterer Strasse 418
53227 Bonn
Germany

Printed in Canada

5   4   3   2   1

ISBN 0-534-35941-8

To my father

About the Author

Edward P. Kardas is professor of psychology at Southern Arkansas University. He has long been interested in applying computer technology to college teaching. Since 1993, those efforts have revolved around the use of the Internet and the World Wide Web in the classroom. Previously, he was coauthor, with Tommy Milford, of *Using the Internet for Social Science Research and Practice*. He is married to the former Julie McCuller, and they have three young children.

Contents

Preface

Overview

How can students use the World Wide Web most effectively? This text makes it easier for students to find entry points into the Web. The text lists nearly 1,100 high–quality Web sites in psychology arranged by topic.

For the Instructor

When Tommy Milford and I wrote *Using the Internet for Social Science Research and Practice* (Wadsworth, 1996), the Internet was much different than it is today. We struggled to find quality sites or URLs (uniform resource locators, the addresses on the Web), for instance. There were not that many social science topical sites. Now, the reverse is true; URLs abound in all disciplines and the task is to winnow out the inferior ones. Also, everyone with access to the Web and a server seems to have created a site. Back then, we assumed that students would easily become efficient searchers of the Web after a little instruction. That assumption was mistaken. It turns out that students have great difficulty in finding worthwhile URLs.

So, this text was written as a means for jump starting students into using the Web. The text does so by providing a large number of stable and informative sites for students to use just by clicking on or typing in the URL. The organization of the text is similar to that of a typical text in general psychology.

This text was written for any psychology student at any level and in any course. To make selection of sites easier for students, each URL listed is described by its title, type of page, depth of coverage, length of page, whether or not it links to other pages, whether or not it contains graphics, and whether it requires additional software. A more complete view of these descriptors is given in Chapter 1. Each URL listed is briefly described as well. In the text, the URL is listed and students must enter it into their browser (i.e., Netscape, Internet Explorer, or similar software). The accompanying CD–ROM contains all of the material in the text and has the additional feature of allowing users to simply click on the URL to see the site when using a browser and a computer connected to the Internet.

Think of this text as a guide to the Web in psychology. Unlike similar texts, this one provides students with a large number of URLs that they can go to immediately to begin learning about psychology. The point here is not to learn about computers, networks, the Internet, or other such subjects. Rather, the point is to have students using the Web to learn *psychology* and to do so quickly. Once students experience some success in actually learning on–line, they should develop the confidence to begin searching the Web on their own. For that is the ultimate purpose of this book: to help students learn how to use the Web efficiently and effectively.

Acknowledgements

Like any text, this one is the product of many people working together. Certainly the discussions between faculty members here at Southern Arkansas University and elsewhere about how best to use the Web have been instrumental in the creation of this text. Tommy Milford and I continue to explore the uses of the Internet and other technology, for example.

New users of the Internet, Joe Bates, John Otey, and Gina Deahl of my department have provided fresh perspectives which were very valuable. Our resident techie, Danny Stewart, served as a sounding board for ideas, from the half–baked to the fully fleshed. Christina Woodruff's work on earlier projects certainly shaped the direction of this text. Students, always the best judges, provided invaluable assistance. Service beyond the call of duty came from my two student workers, Lisa Stevens and Kristi Johnson. They worked tirelessly in the face of my constant demands. I could not have accomplished much without them. Southern Arkansas University's administration and staff distinguished themselves once again. Steve Gamble, president, continues to support my efforts wholeheartedly, and I appreciate that. Ronnie Birdsong is a dear, and she knows it. I certainly know it. Dan Ball and Jerry Pyle do more than they know to aid my efforts. The entire Southern Arkansas family, a term I can use unabashedly, supports me. I thank all of you. Your prayers have helped me much more than you will ever know.

I feel privileged to be a part of the Brooks/Cole and ITP family too. Any author who has been treated as I have would say the same thing. In an age of unanswered letters and e–mail, Brooks/Cole is a throwback to days of grace, manners, and the virtue of hard work. Working with them is pleasure, from beginning to end. Vicki Knight took the time to discuss my project with me at length on the eve of her vacation, and later ended up as my editor after Denis Ralling, my original editor, left Brooks/Cole. Stephanie Andersen performed her usual yeoman duty, answering my calls and e–mail nearly instantly, and smoothing over all of the details necessary to bring the book to completion. Steve Catalano has long been a supporter of my efforts, I thank him too. It is a small world: Michael Campbell, a Southern Arkansas graduate, now executive marketing manager, has done much to aid my success. Finally, the rest of the Brooks/Cole organization, *en masse,* also deserves kudos for their ability to turn ideas into reality so quickly. I must also thank my colleagues who took the time to review the manuscript. Their comments helped shape the final form of the work. Thanks go to: John Anson, Stephen F. Austin State University; William Jack, Franklin Pierce College; David Kreiner, Central Missouri State University; Jeffrey Lindstrom, Fontbonne College; Sherry Loch, Paradise Valley Community College; John Otey, Southern Arkansas University; David W. Wilson, Culver–Stockton College; William Wozniak, University of Nebraska—Kearney; and Christine Ziegler, Kennesaw State College.

Lastly, I cannot say enough for my family. All of them, nuclear and extended, bloodline and in–law, are precious to me. Julie, my wife and soulmate, knows me better than I know myself. Thank you for putting up with me. My children, now augmented by little Cara, are my main source of inspiration. Watching Christian, my seven–year–old surf the Web is an eye opener. Seeing Clay, my youngest son, disassemble and reassemble his transforming toys makes me glad my toys were simpler. Experiencing the joys of observing an infant again is a blessing, as is having a girl to learn from. Thanks also to Lyra and Mike, my mother and brother; and John and Jeanene, my parents–in–law. Their continued love and support are appreciated. Dean, your long–standing backing is, once again, acknowledged. I look forward to you flying in to eat at Dale's soon.

Edward P. Kardas

Locating Web Resources

The World Wide Web grows larger by the minute, so finding Web resources gets harder too. How can students cope? The missions of this book are to get users to start using the Web and to teach them how to find Web resources on their own. Familiarity with computers, the Web, and its basic vocabulary is assumed.

How to Use This Book

Think of this book as a set of entry points into the World Wide Web. Those entry points are designed to follow the organization of a typical general psychology textbook. In the pages that follow are nearly 1,100 URLs (uniform resource locators, the basic addresses of the Web) in psychology. These URLs were carefully selected from more than 10,000 URLs. Each URL listed is summarized to further facilitate searching. So, think of the book as a distillation of many searches for topics commonly encountered by psychology students, faculty, and others.

The easiest way to use this book is to work from the CD–ROM that comes with it. To install it, follow the instructions printed on the sleeve. They will vary depending on the type of personal computer used. Browser software, i.e., Netscape, Internet Explorer, Lynx (if your computer does not support graphics), or other similar programs will be required. An Internet connection, either via a modem or direct, is also required. Then, simply open the files on the CD–ROM from the browser and click on the URLs of interest. Note that both the title and the URL are clickable. In a laboratory environment, check with the lab supervisor before installing any software.

Another way to use the book is to scan it for URLs of interest, and then simply type in the URL carefully into the appropriate box in a browser. **The URL must be typed in exactly, or it will not find the site!** The addresses listed have all been checked at the time of publication and were found to work. Remember that the Web is a very dynamic place, so addresses change or are deleted with some regularity. For errata and new URLs, consult the Brooks/Cole Web page:

http://www.brookscole.com/psychology/authors/kardase/

Any changes or deletions found will be listed on that page. Also listed there will be new URLs found since publication. Users will also be able to suggest URLs they have found and wish included in subsequent editions of this book.

Site Descriptions

The site descriptions that follow have been made in a standard format. Each contains: a **title**, a word describing the **type** of site, the difficulty **level**, its **length**, whether or not it contains **links** to other pages, whether or not the page contains **graphics**, whether or not it contains an internal **search** facility, and whether it requires additional software beyond the basic browser.

1

The title is simply a description of the site. The title listed in this book is usually very similar to the title listed on the page of the URL, but sometimes it is not. Some pages do not have titles; other pages have longer titles. Users of the CD–ROM may click on the title or the URL to have their browser take them to the site listed.

The types of site listed are:

> text—unpublishd writing
> index—collection of links to other URLs
> graphic—photos, diagrams, or other graphics
> interactive—involves user in some way
> tutorial—teaches something about a topic
> article—text from a publication
> animation—movie, QuickTime, MPEG, or other format
> abstract—short description of article or book
> publication—material previously published elsewhere
> book—on–line book
> lecture—lecture notes from a Web course
> FAQ—Frequently Asked Question file
> audio—RealAudio or other format audio file
> download—page has link to download software to user
> journal—on–line journal
> table—material presented in tabular form
> biblio—bibliography

The level description means:

> basic—something every student should know or be interested in
> intermediate (interm.)—more advanced material or more detailed material
> advanced (adv.)—specialized or very advanced material

The length description means:

> short—scroll through one screen or a little more
> medium—scroll through two or three screens
> long—scroll through more than two screens

The links description describes whether or not the page contains links to other items on the page itself (internal links), or to other links on other pages (external links). Use the navigation buttons on the browser and its list of sites visited to move from one link to another and back.

The graphics description tells whether or not the page has any graphics. This descriptor serves two purposes. The first is to provide a gauge of download times; graphics are slow to download. The second is to alert users that they may find interesting graphics related to the topic at the site.

The search descriptor alerts users that the page contains its own internal search facility. Those searches can be very useful and users should take advantage of them.

Some sites require plug–ins, additional software such as Java, Shockwave, RealAudio, and others. Plug–ins provide additional functionality, i.e., animations and audio, typically beyond the capacity of the browser itself. Chapter 3 lists some URLs where such plug–ins may be found. Pages that require plug–ins often provide a link for downloading the required plug–ins. Be aware that some plug–ins will not work on all personal computers. Consult with supervisors before downloading plug–ins in lab settings.

The annotation describes the page briefly. Annotations run from one line to as many as six lines. Users should be able to decide whether or not to visit a site from the annotation. The annotation should be the item of most value to users of this book.

The URL is the actual address of the site listed. Users who type in the URLs must type the URL exactly as listed. Users who use the CD–ROM may either click on the title or on the URL to make their browsers take them to that site.

Searching By Yourself

Eventually, users will want to conduct their own searches. The sites listed below are chock– full of information for doing precisely that. Also, they serve as an introduction to using the book. Read the information in the sites below to learn how to read URLs, use search engines, develop search strategies, and become an accomplished user of the Web.

Finding Information on the Internet—tutorial, basic, medium, links, graphics
Page contains everything a new user needs to get up to speed in using Web search engines. Tutorial covers: terminology, basics of search tools, search strategies, recommended search tools, and much more.
http://www.lib.berkeley.edu/TeachingLib/Guides/Internet/FindInfo.html

Conducting Research on the Internet—tutorial, basic, long, links
Comprehensive site on how to conduct searches on the Internet and the Web. Has links to: a basic guide to the Internet, evaluating Internet resources, directories, the major search engines, and more.
http://www.albany.edu/library/internet/research.html

Getting the Most Out of Earthlink—tutorial, basic, short, links, graphics
Written for subscribers of on–line service, this page provides useful information for beginners and "newbies" about the Internet, the Web, e–mail, Usenet, and other services. http://www.earthlink.net/book/

On Your Own

The next chapter describes one of the big problems of the Web: separating useful information from useless information. Not everything found on the Web is sterling. Users have to develop a sense for distinguishing which sites have solid information and which ones do not. Users do not really "surf" the Web. Better metaphors are "fishing" or "mining." Both of those give a better idea of what searching is all about: finding what is needed in a vast place.

Evaluating Web Resources

The Web gives anyone with a computer and access to a server the equivalent of a printing press. Thus, the Web is full of information—from useful to useless. How can users judge which information is worthwhile and which is not? This chapter will provide some advice on making such determinations.

The Wild Wild Web!

The Web is a wild place. Nearly any kind of information can be found on the Web: from the most explicit sexual materials to serious medical advice; from the rants of adolescents to the work of philosophers; from crackpots claiming the Holocaust never happened to the latest news and weather. How is a user to cope with such a wide variety of information? Fortunately, there are some strategies users can adopt, and those strategies are related methods used in media that antedate the Web.

Questions to Ask

Here are some questions to ask when evaluating Web pages. Remember not to suspend common sense just because the medium is the Web. The same rules apply to any form of media.

- Does the material appear to be accurate? In other words, was it prepared by someone who took care to not make obvious mistakes, i.e, spelling, punctuation, and grammar?
- Who is the author? Does the author identify himself or herself? If not, can one reasonably infer who the author might be? Is the author an authority, a college student, or a high school student?
- Is the material presented objectively, or is there an obvious slant to the information presented? For example, is information about human genetics presented on a page hosted by a white supremacist group? Is smoking and health information provided by a tobacco company?
- How up–to–date is the information? Most search engines will provide the date a page was last updated. Many Web pages will list when they were last updated. Use that information.
- How complete is the information presented? Are there obvious gaps in the material? Is the coverage uniform or are some topics covered in more depth than others?

By answering the questions above, users will take the first step to successfully evaluating Web pages. Users should also remember that the Web is only one source of information. Information found on the Web can and should be checked against information found in traditional media.

Chapter 2

Two–Edged Sword

The Web cuts two ways. On the one hand, the characteristics of the Web, hyperlinks, potential rapid updating or loss of pages, use of other software (i.e., plugins), and search engines, make for an exciting and vital medium. On the other hand, those same characteristics can make problems for users.

Hyperlinks (or more simply, links), the connections that take the user from one URL to another, are one of the unique features of the Web. Links can take a user from one place to another on the same page or from one page to another. Users need to develop an awareness of where they are at any given time. Most browsers allow users to see the URL they are currently reading. That information should be kept in mind when browsing to avoid the "lost in hyperspace" kind of feeling that novice users sometimes develop. Again, most browsers will have navigational aids to help users find where they are currently and where they have been recently.

On the whole, the Web is not a stable publishing medium. Users are literally at the whim of the person who serves the information. Once that information ceases to be served, it is gone, perhaps forever. Some sites, however, are more stable than others. In this text, for instance, sites were evaluated for perceived stability. Many sites with interesting and useful information were not included because they appeared to be unstable. How can users judge stability? One way is to read the URL. Does it have a registered domain name or just an IP number? More than likely, sites with registered domain names will be more stable.

The use of software like plug–ins makes the Web a more interactive medium than print or television, but that software imposes an additional burden on the user. Users may have to download and install the required software., or they may not have sufficient resources on their machines to use such software. Worse still, users without plug–in software may not see all of the information on a page they visit, and so make improper judgments about the page. That is one reason why this text lists what software is required for certain URLs. Notice, however, that most of the pages in this book may be accessed without additional software.

Much of this text was written with the help of search engines. In chapter 1, URLs describing the use of search engines were provided. While search engines are wonderful tools, they can cause problems for novice users. The main problem that novices may encounter is finding pages out of context as the result of a search. Search engines will not take the next step necessary. That step is to determine where the page found came from. In other words, that page may need to be set back into its context. In the writing of this text, that process happened many times. A search engine found a page, but other pages were better suited to inclusion in the text. Those better pages were found by "backing up" the URL found. Here, backing up simply means reading the URL and going back up its directory structure. Backing up the URL is easily done by placing the cursor at the end of the URL and deleting up to each "/" in the URL. Then, by hitting return, the browser will search that new, shorter URL. In that way, higher level pages can often be found, and they often prove to be better than the one found by the search engine.

When users become familiar with the Web, the above strategies will become second nature. Becoming a sophisticated Web user takes time and practice. Part of the purpose of this text is to accelerate that process. Use the sites listed in the subsequent chapters to get into stable and good quality URLs. Later, use search engines and the hints above to find sites.

Resources

Below are listed some resources for evaluating Web pages, finding out who is using the Web, and designing Web pages. The first provides a linked bibliography on how to evaluate Web sites:

> **Bibliography on Evaluating Internet Resources**—biblio, basic, long, links
> Lists Internet resources, print resources, and listservers related to the topic of evaluating resources on the Internet.
> http://refserver.lib.vt.edu/libinst/critTHINK.HTM

The second resource provides information on who is using the Web:

> **WWW User Surveys**—index, interm., short, links, graphics
> The place to find information on who is using the Web and how. Contains links to user surveys of Web usage from 1994 to the present.
> http://www.gvu.gatech.edu/user_surveys/

The third resource is for users who want to design their own Web pages:

> **Web Page Design**—index, adv., short, links, graphics
> This page is for users who want to learn and explore the use of the Web as its own medium. Topics cover nearly all aspects of Web page design and include: typography, graphics and palettes, navigation, and much more.
> http://www.wpdfd.com/wpdhome.htm

Conclusion

The Web takes some getting used to. It shares characteristics of other media, but also brings new capabilities into play. Once users learn the ways of the Web—links, search engines, reading URLs—things become much easier for them. In the chapters that follow comes the true power of this text. See those chapters for a quick entryway into psychology on the Web.

General Resources in Psychology

Resources of general interest to psychologists are found in this chapter. Those resources are arranged as follows: Organizations; Index Sites; Tutorial Sites; Quizzes and How to Study; On–line Periodicals; On–line Texts; Software, Simulations, and On–line Graphics; Career Related; Data Sources; and Just for Fun.

Organizations

American Psychological Association (APA)—index, basic, short, links, graphics, search
Home page of the American Psychological Association (APA), page provides links to PsychNET, student information, member information, and more.
http://www.apa.org/

Links to Individual APA Divisions—index, interm., long, links, graphics
To find information on individual divisions of the APA.
http://www.apa.org/about/division.html

American Psychological Society (APS)—index, basic, medium, links, graphics
Home page of the American Psychological Society, page provides links to information, services, Internet resources, and more.
http://psych.hanover.edu/APS

Office of Teaching Resources in Psychology (OTRP)—index, basic, short, links, graphics
Page contains useful resources for teachers (and students) of psychology. Page has links to resources for teachers, Project Syllabus, *Teaching of Psychology,* and others. http://www.lemoyne.edu/OTRP/

Society for Computers in Psychology (SCiP)—index, basic, short, links, graphics
Home page of a society "... interested in applications of computers in psychology." Page provides membership information, meeting information, call for papers, and a brief history. http://www.lafayette.edu/allanr/scip.html

Index Sites

Psych Web—index, basic, medium, links, graphics, search
Award–winning page in psychology provides a multitude of services and links to information including hints on APA style, quizzes, tip sheets for majors, and much more. http://www.psych-web.com/

Brooks/Cole Psychology—index, basic, short, links, graphics
From the publisher of this book, a site with links to study centers for selected texts, multimedia brochures, catalogs, software demos, and more.
http://www.brookscole.com/psychology/index.shtml

Amoeba Web: Psychology Web Resources—index, basic, short, links, search
This comprehensive site from Southern California College contains links to sites in Applied Psychology, Biopsychology, Career Preparation, Child Development, Cognitive Psychology, Counseling/Psychotherapy, Culture, Disorders, Emotion/Motivation, Gender, General References, Graduate Study, Health Psychology, History of Psychology, Integration, Intelligence, Journals, Language, Learning, Memory, Parenting, Personality, Professional Organizations, Research Methods, School Psychology, Sensation and Perception, Social Psychology, Sport Psychology, States of Consciousness, Statistics, and Testing.
http://www.sccu.edu/programs/academic/psych/amoebaweb.html

WWW—Sites for Experimental Psychology—index, basic, medium, links
Offers links to sites in the following categories: sensation and perception, learning and memory, thinking and problem solving, motivation and emotion, language, neuropsychology, institutes and societies, journals, software, experiments on the Internet, on–line documents, and other starting points.
http://www.psychologie.uni-bonn.de/allgm/links.htm

School Psychology Resources On–line—index, basic, short, links
Large site for school psychology, page has sections for: specific conditions, other information, jobs, and an index.
http://mail.bcpl.lib.md.us/~sandyste/school_psych.html

PsycSite—index, interm., long, links
Large site divided into two major sections: psychology journals on the Net and 29 general categories (subfields) of psychology. http://stange.simplenet.com/psycsite/

PsychREF—index, basic, long, links, graphics
Provides links to general resources, teaching and scholarly activities by faculty, resources for students and academic advisors, and topics and subfields in psychology. Also includes a form for users to provide survey information about themselves. http://maple.lemoyne.edu/~hevern/psychref.html

PubMed—search, basic, short, links, graphics, search
Perform on–line searches of MEDLINE, the database of the National Library of Medicine. http://www4.ncbi.nlm.nih.gov/PubMed/

Psychology Glossary—index, basic, long, links
A linked glossary of common psychological terms.
http://ucnet.canberra.edu.au/~packrat/Psychology.101/glossary.html

Principia Cybernetica Web—index, interm., medium, links, graphics, search
A web index dedicated to philosophy and the eternal questions but with a technological bent. Uses principles from systems theory and evolution to enhance philosophy. Page includes many links to topics of interest to psychologists.
http://pespmc1.vub.ac.be/Default.html

Index of Usenet FAQs—index, interm., long, links
Provides links to Usenet FAQs of all kinds.
http://www.cis.ohio-state.edu/hypertext/faq/usenet/

Serendip—index, basic, short, links, graphics, Java
Site has sections on brain and behavior, complex systems, genes and behavior, science education, and more. Some of the links require Java.
http://serendip.brynmawr.edu/

Upstream: Issues—index, basic, short, links, graphics, search
Page has links to articles on current and controversial issues. Some issues include: evolution, feminism, psychology, and the Bell Curve.
http://www.cycad.com/cgi-bin/Upstream/Issues/

Leading Authorities—index, basic, short, links, graphics, search
Commercial page of a speakers bureau, users can search for psychologists and others who will speak to groups. http://www.leadingauthorities.com/

The Arthur C. Custance Library—index, adv., short, links, graphics, search
Full texts of his books, includes: *The Mysterious Matter of Mind, Evolution or Creation, Is Man an Animal?,* and more. http://www.custance.org/

Hotlist of K–12 Internet School Sites—index, basic, short, links, graphics
Site provides links to K–12 pages throughout the United States.
http://www.gsn.org/hotlist/index.html

NRC Ranking of Psychology Departments—text, basic, long, links
Page lists in rank order the result of the 1995 National Research Council ratings of college and university psychology departments in the United States.
http://www.wesleyan.edu/spn/ranking.htm

Current Topics in Psychology—index, interm., long, links, graphics
Page is a collection of annotated links from other sites, contains articles on topics from addiction to Williams syndrome. Also has links to related Web sites.
http://www.tiac.net/biz/drmike/Current.html

Minerva: History of Ideas On–line—tutorial, basic, short, links, graphics
Page is an "extended glossary" that provides links to: philosophies of nature, theories of human nature, and concepts and thinkers.
http://www.browncat.demon.co.uk/hoi/hoi.htm

Aphorisms Galore—index, interm., short, links, graphics, search
Witty sayings by more than 600 authors, including some psychologists.
http://www.aphorismsgalore.com

Tutorial Sites

ScienceNet—tutorial, basic, short, links, graphics, search
Large database on science that allows users to search the entire database or to search by subtopics. Subtopics are: archeology, chemistry, engineering/technology, environment, earth science, mathematics/computer, biology/medicine, physics/astronomy, and social science. Users may also send in questions that will be answered via e–mail.
http://www.campus.bt.com/CampusWorld/pub/ScienceNet/qpages/search.html

Psych 101—tutorial, basic, short, links, graphics
Basic tutorial on psychology; sections are: people, theory, measures, methods, and links. http://www.psych101.com/main.shtml

Links to Demonstrations and Tutorials—index, basic, short, links
Page provides links to demonstrations and tutorials in several areas of psychology. http://www.smsu.edu/contrib/psych/demos.html

Psychology Tutorials and Demonstrations—index, basic, short, links, graphics
Links to 24 tutorials from a variety of sources, includes: basic neural functioning, mathematical models of memory, social psychology, and others. http://psych.hanover.edu/Krantz/tutor.html

The Psychology Museum and Resource Center (PMRC)—index, basic, long, links, graphics
This page describes the museum at Oklahoma State University. Page contains links to downloadable programs, articles on classroom activities, and other resources. Photos of exhibits are also shown. http://www.cas.okstate.edu/psych/pages/museum.html

ExploraNet—tutorial, basic, medium, links, graphics, search
Interactive exhibits from the Exploratorium in San Francisco. Exhibits change, but old ones are archived. Site includes many exhibits germane to psychology. http://www.exploratorium.edu/

NOVA **On-line**—tutorial, basic, short, links, graphics, search
Page links to individual *NOVA* television show pages. http://www.pbs.org/wgbh/nova/

The Why Files—index, basic, short, links, graphics, search
Site describes itself as "science behind the news," features links to: feature stories, get info, more stories, cool science images, and more. Funded by the National Science Foundation. http://whyfiles.news.wisc.edu/index.html

Educational Psychology—tutorial, basic, short, links
A page of tutorials in educational psychology by Margaret D. Anderson, Cortland College. Tutorials exist for What is Ed Psych?, Behavioral Approach, Cognitive Approach, Humanistic Approach, Piaget, Erikson, Kohlberg, Maslow, Operant Conditioning, Classical Conditioning, Statistics for Teachers, Vygotsky, Facilitated Communication, and Attention Deficit Disorder http://snycorva.cortland.edu/~andersmd/edpsy.html

World Lecture Hall: Psychology—index, adv., long, links
A long list of courses in psychology available in whole or in part on the Web. http://www.utexas.edu/world/lecture/psy/

Southern Regional Electronic Campus—index, basic, short, links, graphics, search
Home page of the Southern Regional Electronic Campus, a consortium initiated by the Southern Regional Educational Board. Users may get information about on-line courses throughout the South. http://www.srec.sreb.org/

Western Governors University—index, basic, short, links, graphics
Home page of the Western Governor's University, an experimental on–line
university. Users may get information about programs and courses.
http://www.westgov.org/smart/vu/vu.html

Quizzes and How to Study

Multiple Choice Quiz Questions for Introductory Psychology—interactive,
basic, short, links, graphics
Self–quizzes for introductory psychology text for: psychology and science, the
human nervous system, states of consciousness, the senses and perception,
conditioning, memory, cognition, animal behavior and cognition, motivation and
emotion, development, individual differences, personality theories, therapies, sex,
friendship, and love. http://beowulf.simplynet.net/ejones/PsyTest/selfquiz.htm

How to Succeed as a Student—tutorial, basic, medium, links
Advice on how to be a college student; topics from studying to housing to work
preparation are included.
http://www.gu.edu.au/gwis/stubod/stuadv/stu_advice_con.html

Overcoming Test Anxiety—article, basic, long, links
On–line version of pamphlet from the Albert Ellis Institute, offers advice on how to
become a better test taker. http://www.iret.org/essays/ota1.html

Psychology Tutorials—tutorial, basic, short, links, graphics
Lists tutorials in psychology, including auditory perception, positive reinforcement,
rhythm perception, and many more.
http://psych.hanover.edu/Krantz/tutor.html

On–line Periodicals

History of Psychology—index, adv., short, links, graphics
Home page of a new APA journal (1998) in the history of psychology. Page contains
instructions for authors, editorial policy, tables of contents, and more.
http://www.WPI.EDU/~histpsy/

HUD Periodicals—index, interm., short, links, graphics
Housing and Urban Development (HUD) page linking to its publications: *Cityscape,
Fieldworks, Recent Research Results, Urban Research Monitor,* and *U.S. Housing
Market Conditions.* http://www.huduser.org/publications/periodicals/

Journal of Memetics—index, adv., short, links, graphics, search, Java
Home page of journal devoted to the study of memes, units of information, in an
evolutionary perspective. Page offers instructions to authors, links to related
resources, and an index of all issues. http://www.cpm.mmu.ac.uk/jom-emit/

Journal of Psychological Inquiry—index, basic, short, links, graphics
Home page of journal devoted to publishing undergraduate student research in
psychology. Page has links to information about the journal, e–mail of editors,
other student journals, student conventions, and teacher conferences.
http://puffin.creighton.edu/psy/journal/JPIhome.html

Behavioral and Brain Sciences—index, adv., short, links, graphics, search
The home page of a journal that publishes articles in psychology, neuroscience, behavioral biology, cognitive science, artificial intelligence, linguistics and philosophy. The journal publishes both "target articles" and extended commentary simultaneously. The page contains instructions for authors, referees, and commentators; a linked list of previously target articles is included.
http://www.princeton.edu/~harnad/bbs/index.html

Psycholoquy—index, adv., long, links, graphics, search
An experimental on–line journal sponsored by APA, it "...publishes short (4,500 word or less) target articles and peer commentary in all areas of psychology as well as cognitive science, neuroscience, behavioral biology, artificial intelligence, robotics/vision, linguistics, and philosophy."
http://www.princeton.edu/~harnad/psyc.html

PubMed—index, interm., short, links, graphics, search
The National Library of Medicine's page to the MEDLINE database which allows users access to more than 9 million citations.
http://www.ncbi.nlm.nih.gov/PubMed/

Science—index, interm., short, links, graphics, search
Home page for the on–line version of *Science,* the journal of the American Association for the Advancement of Science (AAAS). Page contains links to Science NOW, Science's Next Wave, job listings, and advertising.
http://www.sciencemag.org/

Science News On–line—index, basic, short, links, graphics, search
Home page for the on–line version of *Science News.* Contains headlines, selected full–text articles, past issues, and more.
http://www.sciencenews.org/newhome.htm

Scientific American—index, basic, short, links, graphics, search
Home page of popular–level science magazine, site contains links to past issues, exhibits, explorations, and more. http://www.sciam.com/index.html

On–line Texts

Project Gutenberg—index, basic, short, links, graphics, search
A site that links to a massive effort to put books on–line. Page has links to information about the project, e–texts, news, and much more. http://promo.net/pg/

Books On–line—index, basic, short, links, search
Page links to more than 6,000 books published on–line. Page can be accessed by author, title, or subject. http://www.cs.cmu.edu/books.html

Universal Library—index, interm., short, links, graphics, search
Their mission statement is clear: "The mission of the Universal Library Project is to start a worldwide movement to make available on the Internet all the Authored Works of Mankind so that anyone can access these works from any place at any time." Page contains links to FAQ, presentations, and other related links.
http://www.ul.cs.cmu.edu/first.htm

Software, Simulations, and On-line Graphics

PsycLink—index, basic, short, links, graphics, search
Site provides software and Web links for psychology.
http://www.plattsburgh.edu/psyclink/

Software for Psychology—index, basic, medium, links, graphics
Commercial site offering software for experimental psychology primarily. Products are: Alley Rat Pack, Opprat, CC Dog, and the Illusions Pack.
http://www.thecroft.com/psych.html

PsychLab—download, basic, short, links, graphics
Users may download runtime or uncompiled versions of experiments and demonstrations for general psychology. Uncompiled versions require Authorware. The titles are: psychophysics, signal detection theory, Stroop effect, short term forgetting, organization and recall, word superiority effect, decision making, tragedy of the commons, forming impressions, and personality.
http://sunsite.unc.edu/psychlab/

Adobe Acrobat Reader—download, basic, short, links, graphics
For users who need to read .pdf format files.
http://www.adobe.com/prodindex/acrobat/readstep.html

QuickTime—download, basic, short, links, graphics
For users who need to view QuickTime clips on-line or off-line.
http://www.apple.com/quicktime/

Shockwave—download, basic, short, links, graphics
For users who need to view Shockwave enabled Web sites.
http://www.macromedia.com/shockwave/download/

Expersim Project—interactive, interm., short, links, graphics
Users can run simulations: imprinting in precocial birds, etiology of schizophrenia, motivational factors in routine performance, and social facilitation.
http://samiam.colorado.edu/~mcclella/expersim/expersim.html

PsychArt—graphic, basic, medium, links, graphics
Page contains public domain drawings of Adler, Freud, Jung, Rogers, Skinner, Pavlov, and Binet. Site also has links to other public domain image sites.
http://www.sonoma.edu/psychology/psychart.html

Public Domain Images—index, basic, short, links, graphics
Site that offers a variety of types of public domain images.
http://www.PDImages.com/

Smithsonian Photographic Services Home Page—index, basic, long, links, graphics, search
Home page of Smithsonian Photographic Services, contains links to many photos of American history. Includes second Clinton inauguration, the Million Man March, dinosaurs, unsung heroes, and much more.
http://photo2.si.edu/

Blackwell History of Education Research Museum—index, adv., short, graphics, search
A page with links to more than 23,000 images, categories include Hornbook Collection, Battledore Collection, Primer Collection, New England Primer, Speller Collection, Schoolbook Collection, Artifacts Collection, Slide Collection, Sampler Collection, Slate Collection, and Print Collection.
http://www.niu.edu/acad/leps/blackw1.html

Career Related

On-line Career Center—index, basic, short, links, graphics, search
A site where users may search for jobs and upload their resumes.
http://www.occ.com/

Why Have a Resume?—tutorial, basic, short, links, graphics
Site teaches the basics of writing a good resume. Site discusses the reasons for having a resume and takes users through the process of creating a resume in stepwise fashion. http://www.compu-clinic.com/CLINIC/WHYRES.HTM

Data Sources

Statistical Abstract of the United States—index, interm., medium, links, graphics, Acrobat
Provides on-line access to vital statistics of the United States. Statistics available include population, health and nutrition, education, elections, geography and environment, communications, and much more.
http://www.census.gov/prod/www/abs/cc97stab.html

Just for Fun

Braintricks—interactive, basic, short, links, graphics
Features quizzes from book of same title; humorously points out brain "programs" (i.e., power, sex, territoriality) that author says exist in everyday life.
http://www.braintricks.com/home.html

The Journal of Polymorphous Perversity—journal, interm., short, links, graphics
Home page of journal devoted to making light of topics in psychology. Users may subscribe, view sample issue, order past issues, and more.
http://www.psychhumor.com/

4

Psychology as History and as Science

Psychologists have long been conscious of the need to document their history. Perhaps that need comes from a sense of self–consciousness about psychology's status as a discipline. Psychology straddles a wide gulf in academe—from biology to sociology—and psychologists are a varied lot, ranging from hard scientists to humanistic therapists and others. Regardless of their motivation, many psychologists study their past intently. Below are some Web resources that illustrate the breadth and depth of this psychological concern. Because psychology is so historically recent, many of the resources listed below are not, strictly speaking, psychological, but they are all related in some sense to the history of psychology. The resources are arranged according to the following categories: General Resources in Civilization, General Resources in Philosophy, General Resources in Psychology, Ancient and Medieval Development of Psychology, Renaissance and Enlightenment Development of Psychology, Modern Development of Psychology, and Just for Fun.

General Resources in Civilization

OSSHE Historic and Cultural Atlas—interactive, interm., medium, links, graphics, Java, Shockwave
This site has maps and cultural images of Europe and North America. Ancient trade routes, the Greek and Roman worlds, and their successors are covered. The North American portion covers American history through 1860. The cultural images portion covers urban scenes, water use, economic scenes, landscapes, and other categories. http://darkwing.uoregon.edu/~atlas/

Exploring Ancient World Cultures—index, basic, short, links, graphics, search
A comprehensive site covering the following cultures: the Near East, India, Egypt, China, Greece, Rome, Islam, and Europe. The site emphasizes the differences between cultures. http://eawc.evansville.edu/index.htm

World Cultures—tutorial, interm., short, links, graphics
A set of pages on world cultures, includes learning modules, readings, atlases, on–line courses, and other links. http://www.wsu.edu:8080/~dee/index.html

A History of Western Civilization—index, basic, short, links, graphics
An on–line course in Western civilization that includes the ancient world, the Middle Ages, and early modern Europe. The course is broken up into transparency–length segments.
http://www.idbsu.edu/courses/hy101/class.htm

History of the University—index, basic, short, links
A history of the university from the Greeks to now, covers topics from ancient
Greeks to the modern university.
http://quarles.unbc.edu/ideas/net/history/history.html

Ancient Greece Home Page—index, advanced, medium, links
Includes links to original texts, databases, maps, ancient scripts, the Olympic
Games, the oracle at Delphi, and other resources.
http://daniel.drew.edu/~jlenz/grkhist.html

Peloponnese History—graphic, advanced, long, links
This page covers general information, history, tourist information, and maps of
Greece and nearby lands. The history link covers the topic with maps from ancient
times to 1919. Many more maps are available in the map link.
http://vislab-www.nps.navy.mil/~fapapoul/history.html

The Ancient City of Athens—graphic, interm., medium
Page consists of a collection of modern photographs of ancient Athens. Sites include
the Kerameikos, the Agora, the Akropolis, and the Lysikrates Monument.
http://www.indiana.edu/~kglowack/Athens/Athens.html

The Ancient Greek World Index—index, interm., medium, links, graphics
A comprehensive index site that links to land and time, daily life, economy, and
religion and death. Also includes links to a few other related sites.
http://www.museum.upenn.edu/Greek_World/Index.html

Women's Life in Ancient Greece and Rome—index, interm., short, links, search
Index page to information about the life of women in the classical world. Topics are
women's voices, men's opinions, philosophers, legal status in the Greek world,
legal status in the Roman world, public life, private life, occupations, medicine and
anatomy, and religion.
http://www.uky.edu/ArtsSciences/Classics/wlgr/wlgr-index.html

The Philosophy Garden—index, interm., medium, links, graphics
A site dedicated to the philosophy of Epicurus; contains links to information on
him, Lucretius, and Gassendi. Also has links to similar sites.
http://www.c-zone.net/ea/garden.html

Raphael's *The School of Athens*—graphic, basic, medium, links, graphics
A page with several views and details of Raphael's painting in the Vatican. In the
center of the painting, Aristotle and Plato appear to argue. Surrounding them are
many of the luminaries of ancient Greece.
http://www.christusrex.org/www1/stanzas/S2-Segnatura.html

Miles of Styles, Renaissance Art—tutorial, interm., medium, links, graphics
From a larger set of pages on art, this page asks viewers to think about the style
of Raphael's *The School of Athens*. Questions the user about subject and purpose,
artistic effects, history, and culture.
http://www.kn.pacbell.com/wired/art/styles.athens.html

Perseus Project—index, adv., short, links, graphics, search
> Perseus is a "...digital library of resources for studying the ancient world." Perseus has links to art and archeology, texts, secondary sources, help pages, and others. http://www.perseus.tufts.edu/

General Resources in Philosophy

Guide to Philosophy on the Internet—index, interm., long, links, graphics, search
> Site contains Hippias, a philosophy–limited search engine. The site has links to nearly all philosophers of note. Links include: guides, philosophers, topics, associations, journals, teaching/learning, e–texts, bibliographies, mailing lists, newsgroups, projects, preprints, jobs, dictionaries, quotations, miscellany, and Hippias. http://www.earlham.edu/~peters/philinks.htm

Pantheon of Famous Philosophers—interactive, adv., long, links, graphics
> Offers pictures and quotes from a large number of philosophers; allows users to guess the identity of the philosopher. Links to the Department of Philosophy of the Ohio State University. http://www.cohums.ohio-state.edu:80/philo/pantheon.html

Other Philosophies A to Z—text, basic, long, links
> Page consists of a glossary of philosophies and other related terms. http://www.dreamscape.com/willp/phil/evil/other_philosophies.html

Stanford Encyclopedia of Philosophy—index, basic, long, links, search
> This page describes itself as a "dynamic encyclopedia" because its authors maintain its links continously. The page features information on philosophy and philosophers. http://plato.stanford.edu/contents.html

The Internet Encyclopedia of Philosophy—index, adv., short, links, search
> An index page featuring menu selections: timeline, philosophy text collection, key words, and a search. The coverage is both broad and deep. http://www.utm.edu/research/iep/

Bjorn's Guide to Philosophy—index, interm., short, links, graphics, search
> Another index page dedicated to philosophers, this page contains biographies and other information about 27 philosophers. Further, there is a picture of each philosopher and links to other pages of each one. http://www.knuten.liu.se/~bjoch509/

Digital Text Projects—index, adv., short, links
> Site contains full text works by the following philosophers: Aristotle, Bentham, Berkeley, Dante, Descartes, Dewey, Emerson, Hegel, Hobbes, Hume, Kant, Leibniz, Locke, Machiavelli, Mill, Plato, Rousseau, Socrates, Spinoza, and Vergil. Links to similar sites are also provided. http://daemon.ilt.columbia.edu/academic/digitexts/index.html

The Internet Classics Archive—index, interm., short, links, graphics, search
> Offers more than 400 English translations of original Greek and Roman works. Has a provision for user commentary and submissions. http://classics.mit.edu/index.html

Philosophy Page—index, interm., medium, links
A list of texts and definitions of philosophy from Aristotle to World Congress of Philosophy on The English Server. http://english-www.hss.cmu.edu/philosophy/

The Philosopher's Gallery—index, basic, short, links, graphics
Page provides links to pictures of philosophers sorted by country of origin. The site also has links to other information on philosophy and philosophers. http://watarts.uwaterloo.ca/PHIL/cpshelle/Gallery/gallery.html

Pre–History of Cognitive Science—index, interm., short, links, graphics, search
Another page on philosophy and philosophers. Contains links to philosophical and psychological concepts (i.e., associationism, language) cross–referenced to original writings about those concepts. http://humanitas.ucsb.edu/users/cstahmer/cogsci/brain.html

General Resources in Psychology

Today in the History of Psychology—interactive, basic, short, links, graphics
This page allows users to see events in the history of psychology by the date of the year. The page is based on Warren Street's book, *A Chronology of Noteworthy Events in American Psychology.* http://www.cwu.edu/~warren/today.html

Mind and Body: From Descartes to James—index, interm., medium, links, graphics
This page is an on–line version of a catalogue of a book exhibition at the National Library of Medicine in 1992. The exhibition was in conjuction with the celebration of the centennial of the American Psychological Association (APA). Topics include Rene Descartes and the legacy of mind–body dualism, the rise of experimental psychology, and psychology in America. http://serendip.brynmawr.edu/Mind/Table.html

Classics in the History of Psychology—index, adv., short, links
A page with full text works by Aristotle, Baldwin, Cattell & Jastrow, Binet, Cattell, Darwin, Dewey, Freud, James, Koffka, Mead, Plato, Terman, and Watson. http://www.yorku.ca/dept/psych/classics/

Museum of the History of Psychological Instrumentation—index, interm., medium, links, graphics
This page is a digitized version of the 1903 E. Zimmermann (Leipzig) catalog and price list of psychological equipment. It serves as a distant mirror to the history of psychology by exhibiting research equipment of the time. http://www.chss.montclair.edu/psychology/museum/museum.html

Resources in the History of Psychology—index, basic, short, links, graphics
Page offers resources to the study of psychological history, including Bedlam, the National Library of Medicine, and other history–related links. http://198.49.179.4/pages/awalsh/psych-history.html

The History of Psychology—index, basic, medium, links, graphics
Page that links to other resources in the history of psychology. Has links to pages on Dewey, Piaget, Helmholz, Skinner, and others. http://www.guam.net/home/bmarmie/history.html

Biographies of Psychologists—index, basic, short, links
Short biographies of Alfred Adler, Alfred Binet, Edward de Bono, Hans Eysenck, Sigmund Freud, Howard Gardner, Karen Horney, William James, C.G. Jung, R.D. Laing, Abraham Maslow, Don Norman, Robert Ornstein, Wilhelm Reich, Carl Rogers, B.F. Skinner, Thomas Szasz, Lewis Terman, Edward L Thorndike, and John B. Watson. http://userwww.sfsu.edu/~rsauzier/Biography.html#Psychology

The Lifschitz Psychology Museum—tutorial, basic, short, links, graphics
A virtual museum of psychology. Exhibits include history of psychology, psychology in cinema, and anxiety and panic disorders. Other exhibits are under construction. http://www.netaxs.com/people/aca3/LPM.HTM

The FAQ for sci.psychology—FAQ, basic, short, links
This FAQ answers questions about psychology such as: Is psychology a science? How can I do a literature search through the Internet? Nature vs. nurture. http://www.uio.no/~roffe/faq/faq.html

The Scientific Method—FAQ, basic, long, links
From the newsgroup sci.skeptic, this FAQ answers questions about the scientific method. http://www.xnet.com/~blatura/skep_1.html

Library Guide: History of Psychology—bibliography, interm., long
Bibliography prepared for a course in the history of psychology; may be useful to students elsewhere. http://www.slu.edu/colleges/AS/PSY/510Guide.html

APA Division 26 (History of Psychology) Related Resources—index, interm., short, links
This page links to a wide variety of resources in the history of psychology including the Barnard College History of Psychology Museum, *Cheiron* (a journal), and others. http://www.yorku.ca/dept/psych/orgs/apa26/resource.htm

Canadian Psychological Assoc., History and Philosophy of Psychology Section—index, adv., short, links, graphics
Provides information for and about psychologists interested in the history of psychology in Canada.
http://www.yorku.ca/dept/psych/orgs/cpahpp/

History of Psychology—journal, adv., short
Home page of the journal *History of Psychology;* describes journal; provides instructions to authors, and an e–mail link to the editor.
http://www.yorku.ca/dept/psych/orgs/apa26/hpcall.htm

Theory and Psychology—journal, adv., medium, links, graphics, search
Provides tables of contents for past volumes of journal, editorial policy, and instructions for authors. The page also has an e–mail link to the editor.
http://www.psych.ucalgary.ca/thpsyc/

Archives of the History of American Psychology—text, basic, short
This will be the future home page of the archives, a place that already houses materials on the history of psychology in America.
http://www.uakron.edu/archival/ahap.htm

Ancient and Medieval Development of Psychology

The Middle Ages—index, interm., short, links, graphics, audio
A page created by a high school student (at the time), it opens with Gregorian chants. It contains links to materials on the Middle Ages, Stargate experience (a historical fiction account), books on the Middle Ages in the BYU Library, and other Web sites on the Middle Ages.
http://mse.byu.edu/mse/InSci/286/MiddleAges/Intro.html

Aristotelian Universe—graphic, basic, short
Page consists of a color graphic of Ptolemy's geocentric universe. The graphic is from *Cosmographia* (1539). http://aix1.uottawa.ca/~phoenix/apian.htm

Copernican Universe—graphic, basic, short
Page consists of a color graphic of Copernicus's heliocentric universe. The graphic is from *A Perfit Description of the Cælestiall Orbes* (1576).
http://aix1.uottawa.ca/~phoenix/digges.htm

Philo of Alexandria—index, adv., medium
A page on Philo of Alexandria (sometimes called "the Jewish Plato"). Contains many links to information on Philo and his times.
http://www.hivolda.no/asf/kkf/philopag.html

St. Augustine—text, basic, short, links
A biography of Augustine with links to some of his writings (including *Confessions* and *On the City of God*), and to other similar sites.
http://ccel.wheaton.edu/augustine/augustine.html

Angelcynn—index, interm., medium, links, graphics
Anglo–Saxon living history (400 A.D.–900 A.D.). Contains links to various aspects of life in England after the fall of Rome. http://www.hrofi.demon.co.uk/angelcyn/ *or* (USA)–http://www.geocities.com/Athens/2471/

Gaelic and Gaelic Culture—index, interm., medium, links
A page offering information on Gaelic and Gaelic culture, includes links to other similar sites. http://sunsite.unc.edu/gaelic/gaelic.html

***Confession* of St. Patrick**—text, adv., long, links
The full text of Patrick's *Confession*.
http://www.redhat.com/~johnsonm/patrick/patrick.html

The Book of Kells—index, adv., short, links
A simple page linking to three pictures from the *Book of Kells,* an early Irish illustrated manuscript. http://www.tcd.ie/kells.html

Al–Farabi, Avicenna, Averroes—text, adv., long, links
Page provides biographies and information on three early Arab philosophers.
http://www.mq.edu.au/hpp/politics/y67s11.html

On–line Reference Book for Medieval Studies—index, adv., short, links, search
A comprehensive page for the serious student of the medieval ages, this page offers full texts and refereed articles on medieval topics. http://orb.rhodes.edu/

Benedictine History—text, interm., short, links
Page consists of a short page on the history of the Benedictine order. Some maintain that the order's role in the transition from the Dark Ages to the Renaissance was crucial. http://www.css.edu/about/benehistory.html

Plague and Public Health in Renaissance Europe—index, interm., short, links, graphics
This page offers historical and translated manuscripts on the Black Plague, the devastating epidemic of the late Middle Ages.
http://jefferson.village.virginia.edu/osheim/intro.html

Abelard—text, adv., medium
Biography of Abelard, one of the first to challenge the philosophy of realism.
http://www.nd.edu/Departments/Maritain/etext/abelard.htm

St. Thomas Aquinas and Medieval Philosophy—index, adv., medium, links
An on–line book that gives a comprehensive look a Aquinas's attempt to reconcile the teaching of the church with the newly emerging works of Aristotle and the effects of that attempt.
http://www.nd.edu/Departments/Maritain/etext/staamp0.htm

William of Occam—text, basic, short, graphics
A short biography of the author of *Occam's Razor,* one of the first statements arguing for simplicity in explanation.
http://www.hensa.ac.uk/parallel/www/occam/occam-bio.html

William of Occam and Occam's Razor—text, basic, short
Another short biography of William of Occam.
http://paedpsych.jk.uni–linz.ac.at/INTERNET/ARBEITSBLAETTERORD
/PHILOSOPHIEORD/Occam.html

Occam's Razor—text, interm., short, links
A short discussion of the importance of *Occam's Razor* to modern science. Site includes links to other discussions of the same theme.
http://pespmc1.vub.ac.be/OCCAMRAZ.html

Renaissance and Enlightenment Development of Psychology

Francesco Petrarch: The First Modern Scholar and Man of Letters—book, adv., short, links
On–line book (1898) of same title. Contains links to full text selections of his correspondence.
http://don.skidmore.edu/foureyes/english/EVOLVING_CANON/EC_TEXT_FILES
/Petrarch.html

Johannes Kepler—graphic, basic, short, links, graphics
A portrait of Kepler with a link to his biography (in German).
http://www.schwaben.de/home/kepi/f3.htm
Biography (in English). http://www.schwaben.de/home/kepi/bikepler.htm

The Galileo Project—index, interm., medium, links, graphics
Contains an introduction, information about Galileo arranged in a metaphor of the rooms of his villa, resources, maps, a timeline, and student work related to

Galileo. The page also contains a link for text–only browsers. Links lead to a wide variety of information about Galileo, his life and time, and to other scientists of that era. http://es.rice.edu/ES/humsoc/Galileo/

Room IV–Galileo Galilei—interactive, basic, short, links, graphics, QuickTime VR Multimedia version of a room from the Institute and Museum of the History of Science, Florence, Italy. See and read descriptions of an objective lens of Galileo, application of the pendulum to the clock, thermoscope, the middle finger of Galileo's right hand, two of his telescopes, and much more. A QuickTime VR tour of the room is also available. http://galileo.imss.firenze.it/museo/4/index.html

Galileo's Condemnation—text, interm., short, links
The English translation of Galileo's condemnation by the Inquisition.
http://galileo.imss.firenze.it/museo/a/esenten.html

The Sir Isaac Newton Home Page—index, interm., medium, links
An index page on Newton, contains biographical information and links to original works. http://newton.gws.uky.edu/

Bacon—text, adv., medium
Several poems of Bacon's are reproduced.
http://www.shakespeare-oxford.com/baconpoe.htm

Shake–n–Bacon—index, interm., short
A large index page about Francis Bacon, contains biography, full–text original manuscripts, and information on the Bacon vs. Shakespeare controversy.
http://fly.hiwaay.net/~paul/outline.html

Robert Hooke—text, interm., short, links, graphics
This page is a short biography of Hooke and has links to other sources of information about him. Links to related sites are provided.
http://www.ucmp.berkeley.edu/history/hooke.html

Antony van Leeuwenhoek—text, interm, short, links, graphics
This page is on the early Dutch scientist who invented the microscope. Links to related sites are provided.
http://www.ucmp.berkeley.edu/history/leeuwenhoek.html

Leonardo da Vinci—text, interm., short, links, graphics
The emphasis on this page is to da Vinci's theorizing about fossils. Links to related sites are provided. http://www.ucmp.berkeley.edu/history/vinci.html

Leonardo da Vinci: The Search for the Soul Exhibition—index, interm., medium, links, graphics
On–line version of a da Vinci exhibition in London (1996). Contains the contents of six display cases from the exhibit and their related text.
http://www.btfc.org/Leonardo/Leonardo.html

The Hume Society—index, interm., short, links, graphics
Home page of the Hume Society. Contains links to archives, graphics, meeting dates, and other Hume–related information. http://www.oxy.edu/apa/hume.html

A Dictionary of Sensibility—tutorial, adv., short, links, graphics
Page is an attempt to explore 18th century usages of words of sensibility. Words explored are: benevolence, virtue, physiognomy, physiology, landscape, animals, heart, understanding, sense, sympathy, honor/reputation, delicacy/modesty, sublime, fear/terror/horror, imagination, spirit/enthusiasm/transport, character, compassion/pity, wit/humor/invention, communication, community, education, melancholy/madness, and taste.
http://www.engl.virginia.edu/~enec981/dictionary/intro.html

Berkeley—index, interm., short, links, graphics
A page with links to the life of Berkeley, full text copies of his papers, and works about him. The site also has links to other sites on Berkeley.
http://www.maths.tcd.ie/pub/HistMath/People/Berkeley/Welcome.html

A Tour of the Development of Mechanics—index, interm., short, links
The page lists biographical and other information about the following scientists: Descartes, Fermat, Huygens, Newton, Leibniz, Halley, Wren, Hooke, Bernoulli Family, Euler, Lagrange, Fourier, Hamilton, Poisson, Reimann, Faraday, Maxwell, Hertz, and Lorentz.
http://www.chembio.uoguelph.ca/educmat/chm386/rudiment/tourclas/tourclas.htm

Modern Development of Psychology

On Liberty—**J.S. Mill**—index, interm., short, links, graphics
The full text of Mill's (1869) book, *On Liberty*.
http://www.columbia.edu/acis/bartleby/mill/

Auguste Comte and Positivism—index, interm., short, links, graphics
A fully bilingual site (French/English) on the positivist philosopher Auguste Comte, that contains graphics and information on him and other positivists.
http://www.hgx-hypersoft.com/clotilde/

Comte and Positivism—text, basic, short, links, graphics
A brief discussion of Comte's ideas about religion and society.
http://www.stg.brown.edu/projects/hypertext/landow/victorian/religion/comte.html

Carolus Linnaeus—text, interm., medium, links, graphics
Biography and other information about the founder of the classification system used for living things. The site also contains links to other sites on Linnaeus.
http://www.ucmp.berkeley.edu/history/linnaeus.html

de La Mettrie—index, interm., short, links
Page offers links to the full text version of *L'Homme Machine* and to other links on de la Mettrie. http://www.physics.wisc.edu/~shalizi/LaMettrie/

Ernst Mach—text, basic, short, links, graphics
A short biography and graphic of the physicist and philosopher.
http://hawkeye.me.utexas.edu/~heatran/bios/mach.html

The Husserl Page—index, interm., medium, links, graphics
A heavily linked page on the phenomenalist philosopher.
http://www.mesa.colorado.edu/~bobsand/husserl.html

Psychology, Culture, and Evolution—index, basic, medium, links, graphics, search
Page broken into three sections: signs of consciousness (with paleolithic images), cultural–historical psychology, and evolution. The page also has numerous links to related sites. http://watarts.uwaterloo.ca/~acheyne/index.html

Lectures on Philosophers to Physicists—index, interm., medium, links, graphics
Twenty–seven lectures on scientific topics from counting in Babylon to relativity. http://galileoandeinstein.physics.virginia.edu/lectures/lecturelist.html

Eric's Treasure Trove of Scientific Biography—index, interm., short, links, graphics
This site has biographies and pictures of many scientists. Some of the individual scientist's pages are linked to a wide variety of other sites to provide a wealth of information. http://www.astro.virginia.edu/~eww6n/bios/bios0.html

Wilhelm Wundt—graphic, basic, short
A photo (profile) of the founder of psychology. http://www.psy.kuleuven.ac.be/labexp/wundt.html

Wilhelm Wundt and Colleagues—graphic, basic, short
A photo of Wundt in his lab with several colleagues; Friedrich Sander is also identified. http://rpssg3.psychologie.uni–regensburg.de/drosler/research/droeseng/wundt.html

Psychology: Scope and Schools of Thought—tutorial, basic, medium, links, graphics
Six pages about early psychology from a larger on–line course. Covers Wundt and structuralism, James, Freud, behaviorism, and humanistic psychology. http://www.ets.uidaho.edu/levine/u5s1p1.htm

A Translation of Wundt's *Folk Psychology*—text, adv., medium, links
George H. Mead's review (1919) of the English translation of one of Wundt's later works. http://paradigm.soci.brocku.ca/~lward/PUBS/MEAD_068.HTML

William James: Texts—index, interm., short, links
This page provides links to a variety of James's writings in full–text format. http://people.delphi.com/vlorbik/wjtexts.html

William James—index, interm., medium, links, graphics
Page includes many links to information on James. Also includes several graphics. http://userwww.service.emory.edu/~mpajare/james.html

Just for Fun

Hangman for Psychologists—interactive, basic, short
Try to identify concepts in psychology before they hang you. Topics are from C. Alan Boneau's lists in *American Psychologist, 45*(7), July, 1990. http://www.unb.ca/web/units/psych/likely/cgi/hang100.cgi

Psychologist's Crosswords—interactive, basic, short
Thirteen psychology–related crossword puzzles and solutions; users must print out and complete on paper.
http://www.unb.ca/web/units/psych/likely/xwords/xwords.cgi

Psychology Anagrams—interactive, basic, long
Twenty psychology–related anagrams that users can print and solve.
http://www.unb.ca/web/units/psych/likely/anagrams.htm

Biological Bases of Behavior

At the biological end of psychology are a number of fields: neurosciences, comparative psychology, animal behavior, behavioral genetics, behavioral ecology, and others. Unlike other biological disciplines, the focus of the fields mentioned is specifically on behavioral aspects. Students are often surprised at the inclusion of such topics in their first psychology course, but a little thought reveals how relevant the biological bases are to the study of psychology. Web resources are listed by the categories of: General Resources in Biological Bases of Behavior; The Nervous Systems; Researching the Brain; Left and Right Brains; The Endocrine System; Genetics and Behavior; Animal Behavior; Evolution, Ecology, and Systematics; and Just for Fun.

General Resources in Biological Bases of Behavior

BMC Datalibrary Image Index—graphic, basic, medium, links, graphics
Commercially available images of anatomy, physiology, and other categories; includes images of brain, neurons, eye and ear, and others.
http://www.imagesofhealth.com/datalibrary.html

Neuroscience for Kids—tutorial, basic, medium, links, graphics, search
Site with a wealth of basic information on several aspects of the nervous system and the brain. Categories include explore the nervous system, experiments and activities, on–line books and articles, and other related links.
http://weber.u.washington.edu/~chudler/neurok.html

Neuroanatomy and Physiology—tutorial, interm., long, links, graphics
Designed for parents of children with neurological and neurosurgical illness, it contains a lot of basic information combined with color figures.
http://www.bethisraelny.org/inn/anatomy/anatomy.html

Neuroscience Atlas Images—graphic, basic, medium, links, graphics
A collection of images for neuroscience, categories are forebrain, midbrain, and hindbrain, ventricular system, blood supply, spinal cord, and the eye.
http://anatomy.uams.edu/HTMLpages/anatomyhtml/neuro_atlas.html

Neuroanatomy and Neuropathology on the Internet—index, interm., medium, links, graphics
This page has a large number of links to other resources in neuroanatomy and neuropathology. The categories are anatomy, histology, pathology, history, documents, quizzes, books, journals, software, societies, links, about, and new.
http://www.dote.hu/~hegedus/

Neurosciences on the Internet—index, adv., long, links, graphics, search
A searchable site in neuroscience, it covers a wide variety of specialized topics.
http://www.neuroguide.com/

Neuropsychology Central—index, interm., short, links, graphics, search, Java, audio
Site lists neuropsychology links in assessment, cognitive, development, forensic, geriatric, neuroimaging, treatment, and other related areas.
http://www.premier.net/~cogito/neuropsy.html

Neuroanatomy—index, interm., medium, links, graphics
A collection of 16 pages on general aspects of the human nervous system, topics include introduction to the human nervous system, dissection of the brain, limbic structures, diseases of the central nervous system, and others.
http://nan.drexel.edu/nan/neuroanatomy/lectures/lectures.html

Neuroscience Web Search—search, interm., short, links, search
This neuroscience–specific search page allows searches for topics in the biology of the brain and related areas. Be sure to read the search hints for this page.
http://www.acsiom.org/nsr/neuro.html

Anatomical Charts—graphic, basic, short, links, graphics
A commercial site exhibiting a wide variety of anatomical charts including the nervous system, sense organs, and much more.
http://www.anatomical.com/charts/charts.html

McConnell Brain Imaging Centre—index, adv., short, links, graphics
Home page of neuroimaging center, page has links to animations and pictures used for brain surgery and other research.
http://www.bic.mni.mcgill.ca/bic_welcome.html

Anatomical Sciences Index—tutorial, adv., short, links, graphics, Java
Java–enabled images allow viewer to move through tutorials on neurophysiology, embryology, gross anatomy, and microbiology.
http://w3.uokhsc.edu/anatomical_sciences/

Intelligent Systems—tutorial, long, adv., links, graphics
Wide–ranging tutorial on intelligent systems (life, AI), discusses what is life, artificial intelligence, and future directions. Page is heavily linked and a list of Web resources is provided. http://www.cs.brandeis.edu/~brendy/life_sys.html

The Nervous Systems

Organization of the Nervous System—tutorial, adv., long, graphics
Comprehensive tutorial on the basics of the nervous system with line drawings; includes sections on neurons and glia, terminology, subdivisions of the nervous system, peripheral nervous system, spinal nerves, autonomic nervous system, and a self–quiz.
http://www.cc.emory.edu/ANATOMY/AnatomyManual/nervous_system.html

The Neurons and the Nervous System—tutorial, interm., medium, links, graphics
Another tutorial on the nervous system, sections include the basic neuron, electrical activity in neurons, chemical activity in neurons, the nervous system, and others. http://eleceng.ukc.ac.uk/~sd5/research/nn_index.html

Neuron Database—index, adv., short, links, graphics
Page requires free sign–up, and provides tools to study neuronal properties. Specifically, users can study voltage–gated conductances, neurotransmitter receptors, and neurotransmitter substances. http://spine.med.yale.edu/neurondb/

Biochemistry of Neurotransmitters—tutorial, interm., long, links
Part of larger page on medical biochemistry (link on page), this site explains the action of neurotransmitters. Topics are synaptic transmission, neuromuscular transmission, neurotransmitter receptors, acetylcholine, cholinergic agonists and antagonists, catecholamines, serotonin, and GABA. http://web.indstate.edu/thcme/mwking/nerves.html

Bruce's Patch Clamp Resources—index, adv., medium, links
A page for those who would learn and use the patch clamp technique to explore the physiology of neurons, it provides links to specific issues in using this technique. http://electrophys2.ucsf.edu/PatchClamp/patchclamp.html

Aplysia Hometank—index, adv., medium, links, graphics
Provides information for students and researchers interested in Aplysia, the marine mollusk used in neuronal research. http://ganglion.med.cornell.edu/Hometank.html

Explaining Peripheral Neuropathy—tutorial, basic, medium, links, graphics
From the Neuropathy Association, explains the disease peripheral neuropathy. The page also includes links that explain the normal functioning on neurons. http://www.neuropathy.org/explaining/index.html

Symmetry On–line—book, basic, medium, links, graphics
Page is an on–line version of *Symmetry: A Unifying Concept*. Sections include bilateral symmetry, mirror symmetry, the human body, shape and movement; forward motion: bilateral symmetry, imperfect bilateral symmetry; vertical motion: cylindrical symmetry, and spherical symmetry. http://www.shelterpub.com/_symmetry_online/symmetry_home.html

Radial vs. Bilateral Symmetry—tutorial, interm., short, links, graphics
Describes the differences between the two major forms of symmetry found in the animal kingdom. http://www.utm.edu/~rirwin/symmetry2.htm

Self Quiz: Human Nervous System—interactive, basic, medium, links
Self quiz on human nervous system from Psych–Web. http://www.psych–web.com/selfquiz/ch02mcq.htm

The Brain Quiz—interactive, interm., long, links
Users can answer 11 questions about the brain and get instant feedback. http://www.dana.org/brainweek/quiz98.html

Researching the Brain

The Brain: A Work in Progress—article, basic, short, links, graphics
A special report from the *Los Angeles Times,* contains a set of related articles about the brain. Article are: Brain Discovery, Inner Worlds, Conscious Brain, Mental Frontier, and Newborn. http://www.latimes.com/HOME/NEWS/SCIENCE/REPORTS/THEBRAIN/

The Brain: An Interactive Guide and Tour—tutorial, basic, short, links, graphics, Java
The basic function of neurons, the brain, and how the brain compares to a computer are presented. Some pages require Java.
http://fovea.retina.net/~gecko/brain/

The Harvard Brain—journal, basic, short, links, graphics, search
An on-line journal edited by undergraduate students. Contains articles on neurophysiology and other topics. Read current issue or search archives of past issues. http://hcs.harvard.edu:80/~husn/BRAIN/index.html

The External Architecture of the Brain—tutorial, basic, links, graphics
Simply executed tutorial of external anatomy of brain. Provides links to cerebral hemispheres, views of cerebral cortex, the cortex and its layers, division of the cortex into lobes, and specialized areas of the cerebral cortex.
http://www.epub.org.br/cm/n01/arquitet/architecture_i.htm

Brain Model Tutorials—tutorial, basic, medium, links, graphics
Introductory tutorials on basic brain anatomy. Provides tutorials on five separate views of the human brain.
http://pegasus.cc.ucf.edu/~Brainmd1/brain.html

Views of Brain—graphic, basic, short, links, graphics
Page has five color photos of the human brain: left, right, anterior, superior, and inferior. http://rpiwww.mdacc.tmc.edu:80/se/anatomy/brain/

The Whole Brain Atlas—index, interm., medium, links, graphics, search, Java (opt.)
A graphically rich, comprehensive site on the brain; sections on normal brain, cerebrovascular disease, neoplastic disease, degenerative disease, and inflammatory or infectious disease.
http://www.med.harvard.edu/AANLIB/home.html

Introduction to MRI—tutorial, interm., short, links, graphics, search
Covers the following topics: basics of MRI, instrumentation, image characteristics, artifacts, pulse sequences, safety, contrast agents, MR Angiography, MR Spectroscopy, special topics, glossary, and references.
http://128.227.164.224/mritutor/index.html

Human Brain Project—index, adv., short, links
A good source for finding institutions doing research on the brain as part of the project. Institutions participating and their specializations are listed in a link.
http://www-hbp.scripps.edu/Home.html

Lateral Connections in the Cortex: Structure and Function—book, adv., short, links
On-line book about lateral connections in the cortex of the brain, the page consists of a collection of 11 chapters on different views on lateral connectivity.
http://www.cs.utexas.edu/users/nn/web-pubs/htmlbook96/

Sheep Brain Dissection Guide—tutorial, interm., short, links, graphics
This page requires a frames-enabled browser. The page allows students to perform a virtual dissection of a sheep's brain, a common laboratory exercise.
http://academic.uofs.edu/department/psych/sheep/

BrainTainment Center—index, basic, medium, links, graphics
This commercial site sells consumer tests of brain function provides information on brain function. Users may take a simple IQ test on–line.
http://www.brain.com/

The Perspectives Network—index, basic, medium, links, graphics
A page for those involved in some way with brain injuries; provides links to a FAQ (in several languages), reference materials, and other related information.
http://www.tbi.org/index.html

3–D Digital Map of Rat Anatomy—index, interm., short, links, graphics
An atlas of a rat's brain; images are available in two resolution formats: 512x512 or 1024x1024. Users may specify grids and/or labels.
http://www.loni.ucla.edu/data/rat/

ShuffleBrain—index, interm., medium, links, graphics
Contains links to popular science articles, pictures, scientific issues, books, and other brain–related items. http://www.indiana.edu/~pietsch/home.html

The Brain's "Other Cells" Go Awry—article, adv., long, links, graphics
Article about role and function of non–neural cells in the brain: glial cells, Schwann cells, menigeal cells, and others, and what happens when those cells become tumors.
http://www.med.harvard.edu/publications/On_The_Brain/Volume4/Number2
/SP95Awry.html

About Brain Injury—index, basic, short, links, graphics
From a site for relatives and friends of coma victims, this page has links to information on intracranial pressure, understanding coma, the levels of coma, objectives of neurosurgery, a guide to brain anatomy, and a glossary of terms.
http://www.waiting.com/waitingabouttbi.html

Mapping the Motor Cortex—tutorial, basic, short, links, graphics
Two pages that describe the early history of the discovery of brain localization; the first page describes the work of Hitzig and the second that of Penfield.
http://www.pbs.org/wgbh/aso/tryit/brain/cortexhistory.html

Cortex Map—tutorial, basic, short, links, graphics
Discusses and describes the work and location of the motor homunculus.
http://www.pbs.org/wgbh/aso/tryit/brain/mapcortex.html

How Stroke Affects People—tutorial, basic, long, links, graphics
Lists possible effects and symptoms of stroke.
http://www.the-health-pages.com/seniors/stroke/stroke2.html

Atlas of the Primate Brain—index, adv., short, links, graphics
Page contains 63 drawings of various views of the the long–tailed macaque. The page is designed to aid users of MRI images in stereotaxic research.
http://rprcsgi.rprc.washington.edu/~atlas/index.html

Chapter 5

Left and Right Brains

Conversations with Neil's Brain—book, interm., short, links, graphics
In this on–line version, a neurophysiologist and a neurosurgeon describe brain surgery on an epileptic in detail and at length. Emphasis is paid to the laterality aspects of the case. http://www.WilliamCalvin.com/bk7/bk7.htm

The Throwing Madonna—book, interm., medium, links
Another on–line version of a book, here Calvin explores issues surrounding the brain in 17 essays. Several essays touch on issues of laterality. http://williamcalvin.com/bk2/bk2.htm#TOC

Left or Right Brain?—text, basic, medium
A paper–and–pencil test of laterality that can be printed out. The key is provided as are comments about the results. http://www-leland.stanford.edu/~cychen/brain.html

The Split–Brain Student—text, basic, medium
A way that users can simulate the effects of the split–brain operation, requires two participants. http://www.bhs.mq.edu.au/~tbates/321/Split_brain/Split-Brain_exercise.html

Lorin's Left–Handedness Site—index, basic, short, links, graphics
Site answers questions about left–handedness, including prevalence, genetics, longevity, myths, and more. http://watarts.uwaterloo.ca/~ljelias/left.htm

The Endocrine System

The Endocrine System—tutorial, basic, short, links, search
The page gives a basic description of the endocrine system and its glands. http://www.wwf.org/new/issues/endocrine.html

Hormones and the Endocrine System—tutorial, basic, short, links, graphics
Describes the endocrine system and its principal glands. http://www.healthdirect.com/usechk/endocrin.htm

The Endocrine System—tutorial, adv., long, links, graphics
Presents the endocrine system in tabular form, organized by solubility type of hormone. Text describes activity of specific glands: pancreas, adrenals, thyroids, parathyroids, and pituitary. http://trc2.ucdavis.edu/coursepages2/bis10_97/endocrin.htm

The Endocrine Glands—tutorial, adv., short, links, graphics
Provides information about development, gross anatomy, histology; and clinical anatomy of pituitary, thyroid, parathyroid, pancreas, and adrenal glands. Also covers endocrine principles of organization. http://cme.med.mun.ca/~tscott/endo/endotut.htm

Endocrine Self Quiz—interactive, adv., long, links, graphics
Presents anatomical pictures and asks users to find the endocrine glands. Answers are provided. http://rivers.oscs.montana.edu/esg/kla/ta/endocrine.html

Diseases: Endocrine System—index, basic, short, links
Information about diabetes and thyroid disease is presented.
http://www.swmed.edu/home_pages/library/ddc/endocr.htm

The Pherolist—index, interm., medium, links, graphics
Database based on the book *List of Sex Pheromones of Lepidoptera and Related Attractants;* provides information on pheromones and links to other related pages.
http://www.nysaes.cornell.edu/pheronet/index.html

Genetics and Behavior

Primer on Molecular Genetics—tutorial, basic, medium, links
A site from the Department of Energy provides information on topics in molecular genetics. Categories include introduction, glossary, mapping and sequencing the human genome, model organism research, informatics, and impact.
http://www.ornl.gov/TechResources/Human_Genome/publicat/primer/intro.html

Human Genome Project Information—index, basic, medium, links, graphics, search
Page provides basic information about the Human Genome Project. Categories included are news, FAQs, QuikFacts, ELSI * Progress, genetics, assistance, education, publications, acronyms, glossary, links, search, research, and contacts.
http://www.ornl.gov/TechResources/Human_Genome/home.html

The Genome Database—search, adv., short, links, graphics, search
A constantly updated and revised database of human genes maintained in support of the Human Genome Project. Search for: genomic segments, people, citations or other criteria. http://gdbwww.gdb.org/

Human Genome Most Used Links—index, interm., long, links
Comprehensive list of links for resources related to the Human Genome Project includes mapping data sites, sequence data sites, computational biology, and Genome Project best pages. http://www-ls.lanl.gov/HGhotlist.html

Genetics Education Center—index, interm., medium, links, graphics
Contains a large number of links to resources in genetics. Categories are Human Genome Project, genetic education resources, networking, and other information.
http://www.kumc.edu/GEC/

Access Excellence—index, basic, short, links, graphics
Site for high school teachers of biology sponsored by Genentech, a biotechnology company. The site's sections are What's News, About Biotech, Teaching Communities, Activities Exchange, Let's Collaborate, and Classrooms of the 21st Century. http://www.gene.com/AE/

Fact Sheet Index—index, basic, short, links
A series of fact sheets on genetic topics. Categories are Basic Concepts (11), Genetic Syndromes (16), and Individual Perspectives (5).
http://www.boystown.org/deafgene.reg/facts.htm

Electronic Genetics Newsletter—index, interm., medium, links, graphics
Links to 35 articles in genetics. Topics include body hair and intelligence, manic depression, geography and breast cancer, and more.
http://www.westpub.com/Educate/mathsci/elsemain.htm

Ethics and Genetics—index, adv., short, links
Eight articles with commentary about the ethics of modern genetic research, titles include Ethical Issues in Genetics over the Next 100 years, and Choose Better Human Genes. http://www.med.upenn.edu/bioethic/genetics/articles.html

Diving into the Gene Pool—tutorial, basic, medium, links, graphics
From the Exploratorium, teaches about modern genetics and includes sections on ethics, DNA, genetic relationships, sex and inheritance, and others.
http://www.exploratorium.edu/genepool/genepool_home.html

Cytogenetics Gallery—tutorial, adv., medium, links, graphics
Shows what normal and abnormal chromosomes look like under the microscope with different preparations and stains.
http://www.pathology.washington.edu:80/Cytogallery/

DNA Learning Center—tutorial, interm., medium, links, graphics, Shockwave
Provides tutorials in various areas of genetics and biology; some require Shockwave, others may be downloaded. Topics include on–line DNA sequence analysis, and biology animation library. http://darwin.cshl.org/

Animal Behavior

Animal Behavior Sites—index, interm., medium, links, graphics
Page contains a large number of animal behavior links in the following categories: newsgroups, on–line journals, articles and books, education, teacher resources, evolution and phylogeny, and others.
http://www.wam.umd.edu/~jaguar/behavior/behavior.html

Guidelines for Ethical Conduct in the Care and Use of Animals—text, adv., long
Contains the full text of the guidelines for the ethical use of animals in research.
http://www.apa.org/science/anguide.html

National Zoo Home Page—index, basic, short, links, graphics, Java
The home page of the National Zoo, with links to zoo highlights, zoo views, animal photos, friends of the zoo, and a questionnaire. http://www.si.edu/natzoo/

Sea World/Busch Gardens Animal Information Database—index, basic, short, links, graphics
The home page of Sea World and Busch Gardens has links to a variety of information on animals and their behavior.
http://www.bev.net:80/education/SeaWorld/

Species of Mind—book, interm., short, links, graphics
On–line version of book of same title covers the subject of cognitive ethology.
http://www-phil.tamu.edu//Faculty/Colin/SpeciesofMind/

Ethological Experiments—tutorial, interm., long, links, graphics
Summarizes several famous experiments in ethology including Perception Across Species, Tinbergen Experiment on Home Location by Digger Wasps, Fixed Action Patterns, Sign Stimuli, Sticklebacks, Supernormal Stimuli, Baby Schema, Baerends & Kruijt experiment on Position Preference in Egg Retrieval, and others.
http://salmon.psy.plym.ac.uk/year1/ETHEXPT.HTM

Endangered Species Home Page—index, basic, medium, links, graphics
From the U.S. Fish and Wildlife Service; summarizes information on endangered species. Includes lists of endangered species, news, FAQs, and more.
http://www.fws.gov/~r9endspp/endspp.html

Gray's Reef National Marine Sanctuary—index, basic, medium, links, graphics, search
The home page of a national marine sanctuary located off the coast of Georgia; describes the sanctuary and provides a host of educational and research resources.
http://www.skio.peachnet.edu/noaa/grnms.html

Cornell Laboratory of Ornithology—index, basic, medium, links
The home page of the lab includes a newsletter, research summaries, bird song files, and other related resources. http://birds.cornell.edu/

The Honeybee Waggle Dance—text, basic, long, links, graphics
Explains the communication of the honeybee and gives a classroom exercise whereby students can recreate the communication system.
http://insects.ummz.lsa.umich.edu/mes/notes/entnote22.html

Sociobiology—tutorial, interm., short, links
Discusses sociobiology, an approach to studying the behavior of social animals (including humans). Includes link to criticism of theory.
http://galton.psych.nwu.edu/GreatIdeas/sociobiology.html

See the World Through the Eyes of a Honeybee—interactive, interm., medium, links, graphics
Page on how honeybee's vision appears to them (and to us). Allows users to choose a variety of stimuli and then to see how those would appear to bees.
http://cvs.anu.edu.au./andy/beye/beyehome.html

The Boomerwolf Page—index, basic, short, links, graphics
The home page of a particular wolf, page has links to information on wolves and other animals. http://www.boomerwolf.com/

Smithsonian Migratory Bird Center—index, interm., long, links, graphics, search
Page offers fact sheets on migratory bird behavior, the bird of the month, a place to submit sightings, and more.
http://www.si.edu/natzoo/zooview/smbc/smbchome.htm

Evolution, Ecology, and Systematics

The Tree of Life—index, interm., medium, links, graphics
A very long and comprehensive (and still under construction) set of pages that illustrate the relationships of phylogeny.

http://phylogeny.arizona.edu/tree/phylogeny.html

Talk.Origins Archive—index, interm., short, links, graphics
The home page of the Usenet group talk.origins which is devoted to exploring the creation–evolution controversy. Page includes a FAQ and an archive.
http://www.talkorigins.org/

Frequently Asked Questions About Ecology—FAQ, basic, long
A collection of basic questions (i.e., ecology, biosphere, ecosystems, trophic levels, food webs, etc.) relating to ecology.
http://pet.jsc.nasa.gov/alssee/demo_dir/bioblast/faq_dir/faq_ecol.html

Center for Evolutionary Psychology—index, interm., short, links
Home page of the Center for Evolutionary Psychology at UCSB, academic home of Leda Cosmides and John Tooby, two of the founders of evolutionary psychology (EP). Page contains a primer on evolutionary psychology, a reading list, links to places to study EP, and others. http://www.psych.ucsb.edu/research/cep/

Enter Evolution—index, interm., long, links, graphics
Covers Darwin and the theory of evolution. Includes links to topics (3), scientists (25), and UC–Berkeley Museum of Paleontology.
http://www.ucmp.berkeley.edu/history/evolution.html

Charles Darwin—book, adv., short, links
Links to full–text versions of Darwin's *Origin of the Species* and the *Voyage of the Beagle.* http://www.literature.org/Works/Charles-Darwin/

The World of Richard Dawkins—index, adv., long, links, graphics
The "unofficial" home page of Richard Dawkins, author of *The Selfish Gene, The Blind Watchmaker,* and other books about evolution and information. Contains numerous links to related information on Dawkins.
http://www.spacelab.net/~catalj/

Just for Fun

Animal Reasoning—interactive, basic, medium, links, graphics
Page provides short quiz on the behavior of animals in Kenya.
http://www.jambokenya.com/jambo/feature/games/anmquiz1.htm

Grandad's Animal Alphabet Book—interactive, basic, short, links, graphics
An on–line book designed for K–6 students, but it covers basic ecological topics well; includes several quizzes.
http://www.mrtc.org/~twright/animals/english/grandad.htm

Brain Test—interactive, basic, short, links, graphics, Shockwave
A simple but slickly implemented test of laterality. Use for illustration only; not scientifically valid. http://www.wholebrain.com/food-braintest.html

Probe the Brain—interactive, basic, short, links, graphics, Shockwave
Users may explore the motor homunculus of the brain interactively. Clicking on one of 17 areas of the brain will cause the appropriate motor response in the body.
http://www.pbs.org/wgbh/aso/tryit/brain/

6

Sensation, Perception, and Consciousness

How people and animals make sense of the world is the focus of this chapter. Psychology's distant origins lie in this chapter because many of psychology's first questions came from psychophysics. The questions that were answered in the mid–19th century about how the body and brain interpret physical stimuli continue to be of interest today. Newer areas of interest, including sleep, hypnosis, and drug action, also fall in this chapter. Web resources are listed by the categories of General Resources in Sensation; Perception, and Consciousness; Psychophysics; Vision; Audition; The Chemical Senses; Skin Senses; Vestibular System; Kinesthesis; Biological Rhythms and Sleep; Hypnosis; and Drugs and Consciousness.

General Resources in Sensation, Perception, and Consciousness

Brain Briefings—index, basic, short, links, graphics
The Society for Neuroscience provides articles from it journal, *Brain Briefings,* on a variety of topics; brain and nervous system disorders, nervous system repair, the senses, sleep, technology, development, drugs, and brain mechanisms.
http://www.sfn.org/briefings/

Perceptual Change—tutorial, interm., long, links
Tutorial on sensory/perceptual changes due to a variety of conditions: presbyopia, glaucoma, tinnitus, smell, and others.
http://hubel.sfasu.edu/courseinfo/SL/SLtopics.html

Perceptual Processes—tutorial, interm., long, links, graphics
Wide–ranging tutorial on perception covers pattern recognition and attention. Most subtopics have graphic support materials.
http://onesun.cc.geneseo.edu/~intd225/prcptn.html

Neuroscience Tutorial—tutorial, interm., short, links, graphics
Comprehensive tutorial on sensory–perceptual neuroscience: basic visual pathway, eye and retina, auditory and vestibular systems, somatosensory pathways from the body, and more. http://thalamus.wustl.edu/course/

Health Information and Publications—articles, basic, long, links
A long list of public domain publications from the National Institute of Neurological Diseases and Stroke. Covers a wide variety of topics in alphabetical order (from adrenoleukodystrophy to Zellweger syndrome).
http://www.ninds.nih.gov/healinfo/nindspub.htm

Mystery of the Senses: Activity Guide—tutorial, basic, short, links, graphics
A series of simple demonstrations designed to accompany the NOVA program, *Mystery of the Senses.* Activities include smell, taste, touch, hearing, and vision.
http://www.weta.org/eod/mos_guide.html

Internet Psychology Laboratory—interactive, basic, short, links, graphics, Java
Provides information and interactive demonstrations on signal detection, music scale, pitch scaling, illusions, auditory mismatch, and adaptation and constancy. http://kahuna.psych.uiuc.edu/ipl/index.html

Psychophysics

Sensation and Perception—tutorial, basic, short, links, graphics
Short audio definition of sensation and perception. http://www.thomson.com/brookscole/psychology/brochures/nairne/n05b.html

Psychophysics Defined—text, basic, short
Definition of psychophysics from text *Fundamentals of Scaling and Psychophysics*. http://www.psychology.su.se/external/ISP/definition.html

Vision

How We See—tutorial, interm., long, links, graphics
Complete tutorial on the basic processes of vision, also includes links to related classroom activities. http://www.gene.com/ae/AE/AEC/CC/vision_background.html

Important Dates in Vision Science—text, adv., long, links
Page lists advances in vision science from 1600 to 1960. A link to pre–1600 work is also provided. http://www.socsci.uci.edu/cogsci/vision/yellott_dates.html

Eye Diagram—graphic, basic, short, graphics
3-D color–labelled diagram of the human eye. http://www.cs.ucf.edu/~ceh/Government/gov2/SessionC/eye.html

Visionary—tutorial, adv., short, links, graphics
An on–line dictionary for terms used in the study of human and animal vision, includes feedback links and appendices on cortical areas, Grossberg, and Marr. http://cns-web.bu.edu/pub/laliden/WWW/Visionary/Visionary.html

Cow Eye Dissection—interactive, basic, short, links, graphics
Audio requires Real Audio Player; step–by–step guide for dissection of cow eye. http://www.exploratorium.edu/learning_studio/cow_eye/index.html

Procedures for Vision Problems and Corrections—tutorial, basic, medium, links, graphics
Commercial page about type of corrective eye surgery, but also explains nearsightedness, farsightedness, focusing, and astigmatism. http://www.lca-vision.com/b_procs.html

Stereogram FAQ—FAQ, basic, medium, links
Explains single–image random–dot stereograms (SIRDS); and answers questions about them. http://sancy.ensieta.fr/~lecontcy/sirds_faq.html

The Joy of Visual Perception—book, basic, short, links, graphics
Comprehensive on–line book on visual perception. Covers all of the major aspects of visual perception. http://www.yorku.ca/eye/

IllusionWorks— interactive, basic, medium, links, graphics, search, Java, Shockwave
Illusions are covered systematically. The Hall of Illusions section contains Impossible Figures and Objects, Ambiguous Illusions, Distortion Illusions, Aftereffects and Afterimages, Auditory Illusions, and Camouflage. Other sections cover art illusions, puzzles, and 3–D illusions. Java and Shockwave are required to see some of the demonstrations. http://www.illusionworks.com/

Escalator Up or Down?—graphic, basic, short, graphics
A computer–enhanced image made more ambiguous: Is the escalator going up or down? http://www.geog.le.ac.uk/argus/About/People/Kath_Stuff/edgesbw2.jpg
Compare to original photo.
http://www.geog.le.ac.uk/argus/About/People/Kath_Stuff/stairsbw.jpg

Visual Illusions Gallery—index, basic, short, links, graphics
Presents 21 illusions including: Necker Cube, Afterimages, The Blind Spot, and others. http://valley.uml.edu/landrigan/ILLUSION.HTML

Vision Science—index, basic, short, links, graphics
Comprehensive index page on vision research. Page contains links to FAQs, conference information, labs and research groups, jobs, journals, and much more. http://www.visionscience.com/

The Munsell System of Color Notation—text, interm., medium, links, graphics
Describes the Munsell system for describing colors; has links to history of system and to products available including tests of color vision.
http://www.munsell.com/munsell1.htm

Vision Test—interactive, basic, short, links, graphics
A vision test users can take from their computer screen.
http://www.milfordeye.com/vtest.htm#chart

Interactive Illustrations of Color Perception—interactive, interm., medium, links, graphics, Java
Provides interactive examples of how colors interact with surfaces and with each other.
http://www.cs.brown.edu/research/graphics/research/illus/spectrum/home.html

Distilled Light—interactive, basic, short, links, graphics
On–line demonstration of how primary colors can be combined to form secondary colors. Users may block primary colors and see the results.
http://www.exploratorium.edu/imap-expl/interf.conf?319,66

The Synesthetic Experience—index, interm., short, links, graphics
Page attempts to describe the phenomenon of synesthesia. Links include Synesthete Perspectives, Virtual Synesthesia (demos), and Readings/References.
http://web.mit.edu/synesthesia/www/synesthesia.html

Experiments in Visual Thinking—interactive, basic, medium, links, graphics
Page allows users to perform mental rotations on–line. Similar to Shepard and Metzler's (1971) research that demonstrated that the closer the rotation was to 180 degrees the longer it took participants to perform the rotation.
http://www.sv.vt.edu/class/esm5984/GenInfo/Gen_Prin/viz_exp/exp_viz_think.html

Audition

Acoustical Society of America—index, basic, short, links, graphics
Home page of the society page contains links to information about the society and to a page of sounds (bugle, whales, cymbal, and others). http://asa.aip.org/

Ear Diagram—graphic, basic, short, links, graphics
From the company that created images for the *World Book Encyclopedia,* here is a color diagram of the ear. http://www.van-garde.com/Encyclopedia_1/Ear.html

Introduction to Cochlear Mechanics—tutorial, intermediate, short, links, graphics
Tutorial on the cochlea and its action: location of the cochlea, inside the cochlea, physiological measurements, outer hair cell motility, the cochlear amplifier, and traveling waves. http://www.boystown.org/cel/cm_intro.htm

Cochlear Fluids—tutorial, basic, medium, links, graphics
Tutorial on the fluids in the cochlea: fluid in your ears, anatomy of the inner ear, cochlear anatomy, cochlear fluids composition, and endolymphatic hydrops. Page also has links to other ear–related sites. http://oto.wustl.edu/cochlea/

Cochlear Implant—graphic, basic, short, links, graphics
From the company that created this image for the *World Book Encyclopedia,* here is a color diagram of a cochlear implant. http://www.van-garde.com/Encyclopedia_1/Cochlear.html

Tinnitus Fact Sheet—index, basic, medium, links
From a tinnitus clinic; answers questions about and suggests therapy for "ringing in the ears." http://www.ohsu.edu/ohrc/tinnitusclinic/fact_sheet.html

Hearnet—index, basic, short, links, graphics
Home page of Hearing Education and Awareness for Rockers (HEAR). Promotes the use and sale of hearing protection for rock and roll musicians. http://www.hearnet.com/text/mainframe.html

Otolaryngology Health Questions—FAQ, basic, short, links, graphics
Provides answers to ear, nose, and throat health questions: tonsils and adenoids, ear disorders, snoring, and sleep apnea and others. http://weber.u.washington.edu/~otoweb/factsheet.html

Interactive Overview of Temporal Bone Anatomy and Pathology—interactive, adv., short, links, graphics, search, Java
Uses MRI images for tutorial in the anatomy of the temporal bone; offers choices of search, atlas, electronic text (Java req.), and other options. http://206.39.77.2/temporalbone/Temporal_home.html

Role of Eustachian Tubes—tutorial, basic, short, links, graphics
The role and function of the eustachian tube is explained. http://www.healthnet.ivi.com/hnews/9611/htm/ww5rk85.htm

Spectrogram Reading—tutorial, adv., short, links, graphics
Defines waveforms, phonemes, and spectrograms; teaches how to "read" spectrograms. http://www.cse.ogi.edu/CSLU/cse551/

Haskins Laboratories—index, interm., medium, links, graphics
Demonstrates and explains old and current research in audition: pattern playback, articulatory synthesis, sine wave synthesis, gestural computational model, and the vocal tract visualizer. All research shown has an associated demonstration. http://www.haskins.yale.edu/Haskins/MISC/special.html

X–ray Film Database for Speech Research—animation, adv., medium, links, graphics
This page has information about the research technique of using x–rays to image speakers as they talk. Page contains three examples of such x–ray films in both still and moving formats.
http://www.haskins.yale.edu/Haskins/TIEDE/database.html

A 5–Minute Hearing Test—text, basic, medium, links
Provides a self–administered (except for the last question) test of hearing.
http://www.ramseymed.org/entspecialty/htest.htm

Tone Memory—audio, basic, short, links, graphics
A demonstration where users can judge the differences between two tones in several ways. Also has audio explanation available.
http://www.exploratorium.edu/imap-expl/interf.conf?70,205

Hearing and Balance—tutorial, short, interm., links, graphics
On–line course's page on hearing and balance includes links to detailed material on ears, hearing, and balance. http://www.neurophys.wisc.edu/h&b/index.html

The Chemical Senses

Chemical Senses—journal, adv., short, links, graphics, search
Home page of the journal *Chemical Senses* has links to search of current and previous volumes and information for contributors and subscribers.
http://www.oup.co.uk/jnls/list/chemse/

Monell Chemical Senses Center—index, interm., short, links, graphics
Home page of interdisciplinary research center in the chemical senses; basic information on the psychophysiology of smell, taste, and chemosensory irritation.
http://www.monell.org/

Smell—text, basic, short, links
Smelling and problems with smelling are defined in this page from the National Institute on Deafness and Other Communication Disorders.
http://www.nih.gov/nidcd/smell.htm

Taste and Smell—tutorial, interm., long, links, graphics
Basic information with diagrams on the gustation and olfactory systems.
http://www.umds.ac.uk/physiology/jim/tasteolf.htm

Smell and Taste Disorders—FAQ, basic, medium, links
A set of questions and answers about smell and taste disorders from the National Institute on Deafness and Other Communication Disorders.
http://www.nih.gov/nidcd/smltaste.htm

Smell and Taste Disorders—text, basic, medium, links
Provides more basic information on normal and abnormal aspects of smell and taste from the American Academy of Otolaryngology.
http://www.netdoor.com/entinfo/smellaao.html

The Claims of Aroma Therapy—article, basic, long, links
Article from *The Skeptical Inquirer* (May, 1996) questions the claims of aroma therapy. http://www.csicop.org/si/9605/aroma.html

The Vomeronasal Organ—tutorial, adv., long, links, graphics
The mammalian vomeronasal organ's structure and function are explained. Page contains a picture and references. http://www.neuro.fsu.edu/research/vomer.htm

Skin Senses

Touch Perception—tutorial, interm., long, links, graphics
Comprehensive tutorial with graphics on the skin senses; discusses touch, proprioceptive sensations, pain, and thermal sensations. Also includes graphic of sensory homunculus and table of skin sensitivity by body location.
http://www.science.mcmaster.ca/Psychology/psych2e03/lecture11/touch.le cture.html

Pain Imaging Lab—animation, interm., short, links, graphics, QuickTime, MPEG
Index to animations and pictures of the brain during acute and chronic pain; requires QuickTime or MPEG viewing software. Page also has links to other related resources on pain. http://128.231.106.172/DIRweb/NAB/coghill.htm

Questions and Answers About Pain Control—FAQ, basic, short, links, graphics
Provides answers to seven common questions about pain and its control.
http://pain.roxane.com/library/PatientLibrary/NCI/ncic6.html

What is Phantom Limb Pain?—text, basic, short, links
Description of symptoms of phantom limb.
http://www.mediconsult.com/general/shareware/pain_control/what_1.html

Referred Pain—text, basic, short, links
List of sites of pain origin and where on the body they are referred.
http://icakusa.com/healthcaps/referred.htm

Vestibular System

The Vestibular System—tutorial, basic, short, links, graphics
Five linked pages on the anatomy and function of the human vestibular system, includes animation of pathway of the vestibular–ocular reflex.
http://132.206.103.223/lab/vestib1.htm

Vestibular Disorders Association—index, basic, short, links, graphics
Home page of support group for patients with vestibular problems. Links include vestibular disorders, Meniere's disease, labyrinthitis and neuronitis, and others.
http://www.teleport.com/~veda/index.shtml

Motion Interpretation—article, interm., long, links
Describes how the body reacts to motion: introduction, review of the ear, proprioceptive kinetic sensations, motion sickness, summary, and references.
http://www.ispub.com/journals/IJAMT/Vol1N1/motion.htm

Aviation/Aerospace Medicine Articles and Publications—index, interm., short, links
Page contains articles on the physiology and perception of flying. Titles include Spatial Orientation and Disorientation during Flight, Approach and Landing Illusions, False Climb Illusion in Flying, and many others.
http://www.ozemail.com.au/~dxw/avmedpub.html

Kinesthesis

Proprioception, Kinesthesia, and Motor Reflexes—tutorial, interm., long, links, graphics
Page covers nearly all aspects of proprioception, kinesthesia, and motor reflexes. Has color graphics included with its explanations.
http://nan.drexel.edu/nan/neuroanatomy/lectures/lec12b/lec12b.html

Biological Rhythms and Sleep

Biological Rhythms: Overview—text, adv., long, links
Presents basic information on circadian rhythms, lists basic research issues, and provides a reading list. http://www.sfu.ca/~mcantle/biorhyth.html

Circadian Rhythms—tutorial, basic, medium, links, graphics, search
Presents basic information about circadian rhythms and jet lag. Has link to page of suggestions for avoiding jet lag and problems caused by night work.
http://www.mayohealth.org/ivi/mayo/9503/htm/circadia.htm

Time Jumps—tutorial, basic, short, links, graphics
Personal advice from William H. Calvin on how to avoid jet lag.
http://weber.u.washington.edu/~wcalvin/timejump.html

SleepNet—index, basic, short, links, graphics
Covers a number of aspects of sleep. Includes links to sleep disorders, research, dreams, professional organizations, sleep labs, and other related links.
http://www.sleepnet.com/index.shtml

Yahoo! Science: Psychology: Sleep and Dreams—index, basic, short, links, graphics, search
Results of Yahoo! search on sleep and dreams includes 26 links.
http://www.yahoo.com/Science/Psychology/Sleep_and_Dreams

Sleep Home Pages—index, basic, short, links, graphics
Indexes a number of sites concerned with sleep includes molecular biology of sleep, new abstracts and papers in sleep, discussion forums, and more.
http://bisleep.medsch.ucla.edu/

Sleep and Dreams—index, basic, short, links, graphics
An index page from MegaPsych has 13 links to sites on sleep and dreaming.
http://www.tulsa.oklahoma.net/~jnichols/snd.html

The Quantitative Study of Dreams—index, adv., short, links, graphics, search
Home page of research group that studies dreams objectively and quantitatively; sections include findings, example dreams, coding rules, resources for scientists, and more. http://zzyx.ucsc.edu/~dreams/index.html

A Good Night's Sleep—text, basic, medium, links, graphics
Describes basic facts about sleep and provides hints for getting a good night's sleep. http://www.medaccess.com/seniors/agepg/ap01.htm

Sleep, Dreams, and Wakefulness—index, basic, short, links, graphics, search
Page covers topics in sleep and wakefulness including Articles, What's New, and links to related resources. http://ura1195-6.univ-lyon1.fr/index_e.html

Sudden Infant Death and Other Infant Death—index, basic, medium, links, graphics, search
Comprehensive index page on SIDS/OID: SIDS information, FAQs, pregnancy and infant loss, and others. http://sids-network.org/

Seasonal Affective Disorder—text, interm., long, links
Report of a talk by Norman E. Rosenthal, M.D., a pioneer in the discovery and treatment of seasonal affective disorder (SAD). Describes the history and treatment of SAD.
http://infonet.welch.jhu.edu/departments/drada/articles/articl10.htm

Hypnosis

The Reality of Hypnosis—text, adv., long, links
Long exposition on hypnosis by Joseph Barber, a leading expert. Includes sections on what is hypnosis, how does it work, who can be hypnotized, and others.
http://goinside.com/97/4/barber.html

Hypnosis and Memory—index, basic, short, graphics
Links to general facts about hypnosis and memory, general studies on hypnosis and memory, hypnosis and memory in the forensic recovery of memories, and literature on hypnosis and memory.
http://www.guam.net/home/bmarmie/hypnosismem/hypmem.html

Drugs and Consciousness

Drugs and Behavior Links—index, basic, long, links
Comprehensive page of links to topics in drugs and behavior. Topics include placebos, sedatives, inhalants, alcohol, analgesics and opiates, stimulants, hallucinogens, marijuana, and others.
http://www.uwsp.edu/acad/psych/tdrugs.htm

Alcohol and Substance Abuse—index, basic, short, links
Links to pages on alcohol, amphetamines, anabolic steroids, caffeine, cocaine (crack), hallucinogens, heroin, hypnotics/sedatives, inhalants, marijuana (Cannabis), morphine, prescription drugs, and more.
http://web.bu.edu:80/COHIS/subsabse/subsabse.htm

Orphans of Addiction—article, basic, short, links, graphics
Special report on drug–linked child abuse in California; article includes photos and links to related stories.
http://www.latimes.com/HOME/NEWS/REPORTS/ORPHANS/

Web of Addictions—index, basic, short, links, graphics
Page provides links to resources in addictions of all types. Includes links to facts, meetings, help, and others. http://www.well.com/user/woa/

On–line AA Recovery Resources—index, basic, long, links, graphics
Provides links to resources from Alcoholics Anonymous (AA): information about Alcoholics Anonymous, non–English language AA resources, AA literature, regional AA resources, convention and event information, AA–related computer programs, links to more AA–related resources, and more. http://www.recovery.org/aa/

Alcoholics Anonymous (AA)—index, basic, short, links, graphics
Home page of Alcoholics Anonymous users may select English, Spanish, or French versions of the page. Provides basic information about AA.
http://www.alcoholics-anonymous.org/index.html

Self–scoring Alcohol Check Up—interactive, basic, short, links
Short quiz for determining severity of drinking problems; page scores itself automatically. http://www.cts.com/crash/habtsmrt//chkup.html

Marijuana Anonymous—index, basic, short, links, graphics
Home page of group offers advice and information on how to quit smoking marijuana. http://www.marijuana-anonymous.org/

Cocaine Anonymous—index, basic, short, links, graphics
Home page of group offers advice and information on how to quit cocaine addiction. http://www.ca.org/

Blair's Quitting Smoking Resources—index, basic, short, links, graphics
Page contains information about how to quit smoking. Links include a chat room, bookstore, tools, and links to related resources.
http://www.chriscor.com/linkstoa.htm

7

Learning and Conditioning

Learning is where the roots of modern psychology lie. When American psychology reinvented itself in the second and third decade of the 20th century, research in learning led the way. More recently and under the influence of cognitive research, the study of learning has changed. It has become less mechanistic and more accepting of cognitive explanations, for instance. Learning still is a major part of psychology because of the importance of learned behaviors in the life of human beings. Below are listed URLs of interest to students of learning. The URLs are grouped by the categories of General Resources in Learning; Classical Conditioning and Operant Conditioning; Biological and Cognitive Effects; Observational Learning; Behavior Modification; and Just for Fun.

General Resources in Learning

JEAB—journal, adv., short, links, graphics, search, Java
Journal of the Experimental Analysis of Behavior home page features current issue, previous issues, selected reprints, abstract search, audio and visual material, announcements, instructions for contributors, and more.
http://www.envmed.rochester.edu/wwwrap/behavior/jeab/jeabhome.htm

JABA—journal, adv., short, links, graphics, search, Java
Journal of Applied Behavior Analysis home page features current issue, previous issues, selected reprints, abstract search, audio material, announcements, instructions for contributors, and more.
http://www.envmed.rochester.edu/wwwrap/behavior/jaba/jabahome.htm

The Behavioral System—tutorial, basic, medium, links
Discusses types of learning and some basic terms and concepts.
http://www.valdosta.peachnet.edu/~whuitt/psy702/behsys/behsys.html

ABA—index, adv., short, links, graphics
The home page of the Association for Behavioral Analysis provides membership information, links to special interest groups, the annual convention, and more.
http://www.wmich.edu/aba/

Balance—publication, adv., long, links, graphics
An on–line newsletter published by the ABA (see above); strives to secure an accurate representation of behavioral analysis between the profession and the public. http://www.onlearn.com/balance.html

Explorations in Learning and Instruction—index, interm., short, links
Menu–driven linked database covering 50 theories of learning and instruction. Users may browse by theories, learning domains, or learning concepts. http://www-hcs.derby.ac.uk/tip/index.html

Behaviorism—tutorial, adv., long, links
Tables list theoretical issues in behaviorism. Tables are: criticisms and responses to behaviorist arguments, behavioral data language, theoretical concepts, theorizing, S–R psychology, and the organization of behavior.
http://galton.psych.nwu.edu/GreatIdeas/behaviorism.html

Definitions of Behaviorism—text, interm., long
Classroom hand out describes, characterizes, and contrasts methodological behaviorism with radical behaviorism.
http://www.uwm.edu/People/jcm/psy551/skinner.2/ho2

Behavior Analysis, Radical Behaviorism, Mentalism, and Methodological Behaviorism—text, adv., long
Classroom handout fully characterizes and describes behavior analysis and radical behaviorism. The issue of mentalism is addressed and behavior analysis's objections to it are explained.
http://www.uwm.edu/People/jcm/psy551/skinner.2/ho3

Classical Conditioning and Operant Conditioning

Behavior Terminology—text, basic, long, links
Page provides a list of basic terms use in describing learning and conditioning, a self test, and more information about learning and conditioning.
http://pages.prodigy.com/behavior/

Lectures in Learning—index, basic, short, links, graphics
From the home page of an instructor; provides basic, referenced lectures with graphics: evolution and animal intelligence, the reflex from Descartes to Pavlov, basic concepts in classical conditioning, cognitive models of associative learning, what is learned in classical conditioning, trial and error, from the rise of Thorndike to the fall of J.B. Watson, operant conditioning, generality, constraints and concepts in learning. http://www.dur.ac.uk/~dps1rwk/

Classical Conditioning—tutorial, interm., short, links, graphics
Tutorial covers factors determining the effectiveness of classical conditioning, Resocorla–Wagner model, where are associations made, and what are associations made between.
http://www.biozentrum.uni-wuerzburg.de/~brembs/classical/classical.html

Classical Conditioning of Proboscis Extension in Honeybees—interactive, adv., long, links, graphics
Complete instructions (with photos) on how to perform a classical conditioning experiment using honeybees.
http://www.cas.okstate.edu/psych/faculty/abramson/beeexperiment1.html

Classically Conditioning Earthworms—interactive, interm., medium, links, graphics
Complete instructions (with photos) on how to perform a classical conditioning experiment using earthworms. Simpler than the one above using bees above.
http://www.cas.okstate.edu/psych/faculty/abramson/worms.html

Operant or Instrumental Conditioning—tutorial, basic, long, links, graphics
Page covers the basics of operant and instrumental conditioning. Topics include early investigation of instrumental conditioning, some terminology, some characteristics of operant conditioning, Premack's principle, positive and negative reinforcement, and avoidance learning.
http://www.general.uwa.edu.au/u/kraepeln/operant.htm

Operant/Respondent Distinction—tutorial, interm., long
A classroom handout on the differences between operants and respondents (classical conditioning). http://www.uwm.edu/People/jcm/psy551/skinner.1/ho3

Rat in a Skinner Box (operant chamber)—graphic, basic, short, graphics
Color photo of a white rat in a Skinner box.
http://www.sigmaxi.org/amsci/captions/captions96-03/blum-2.html

Pigeon in a Skinner Box (operant chamber)—graphic, basic, short, graphics
Color graphic of a pigeon in a Skinner box.
http://www.sigmaxi.org/amsci/img/Art95-05/Wasserman.gif

Positive Reinforcement—tutorial, basic, long, links
Page teaches the concept of positive reinforcement, provides a definition and six examples. http://server.bmod.athabascau.ca/html/prtut/reinpair.htm

Reinforcement and Punishment—tutorial, interm., long
A classroom handout on the definitions of reinforcement and punishment; and the details and nuances of positive and negative aspects of both.
http://www.uwm.edu/People/jcm/psy551/skinner.1/ho2

Learning—tutorial, basic, short, links, graphics
Page from an on–line course covers three aspects of learning: classical conditioning, operant conditioning, and cognitive learning.
http://www.science.wayne.edu/~wpoff/memory.html

Animal Training at Sea World—index, basic, short, links, graphics
Page about how marine mammals are trained at Sea World. Topics include introduction to animal behavior, introduction to animal training, how animals learn, marine mammal training at Sea World, the Sea World auditory cueing system, why do we train animals, bibliography, and books for young readers.
http://www.seaworld.org/animal_training/atcontents.html

The Annual Skinner Box Competition—text, interm., long, links, graphics
Student project directions for constructing and conditioning a rat in a Skinner Box (operant chamber). Page is for teachers of high school science project students, but can be read by anyone interested in the mechanics of operant conditioning.
http://www.gene.com/ae/AE/AEC/AEF/1996/banister-marx_rat.html

Ask Judy's Rat—text, basic, short, links, graphics
Page tells the story of a rat trained to wire schools for the Internet by going through existing conduit while holding a string in its mouth. The string is attached to Category 5 cable. The page has links to stories and graphics about the rat.
http://www.judyrat.com/

Rat Lab—text, adv., long, links, graphics
How to condition rats in a Skinner Box (operant chamber); from a course in experimental psychology. Provides the details for such activity.
http://www.furman.edu/~jearles/ratlab.html

B. F. Skinner's Bibliography—biblio., adv., long, links, graphics
Lists all of Skinner's publications and has links to his books (with descriptions), free reprints, and to the B. F. Skinner Foundation home page.
http://www.lafayette.edu/allanr/biblio.htm

The Hullian Approach to Learning—text, basic, long
This page briefly describes Clark Hull's approach to learning and some of the data that failed to support his drive–reduction hypothesis.
http://www.uwm.edu/People/jcm/psy551/hull/ho2

Spence's Modifications of Hull's Approach—text, adv., long
Spence's attempts to account for the PRE, cognitive factors in learning, latent learning, and other phenomena are covered in this classroom handout.
http://www.uwm.edu/People/jcm/psy551/spence/ho2

Biological and Cognitive Effects

Misbehavior—tutorial, interm., medium, links, graphics
Page discusses the conflict between conditioning and biological constraints on learning. Page is heavily linked and is part of a course in learning and conditioning. Some parts of the course require Java and registration for access.
http://www.users.csbsju.edu/~tcreed/pb/misbehav.html

Instinctive Drift and Preparedness—text, basic, short
Short summary of Breland's research and conclusions about instinctive drift.
http://www.macalester.edu/~psych/whathap/diaries/diariesf95/Sarah/bre
lands.html

Autoshaping/Automaintenance—text, interm., long
Complete explanations of the phenomenon of autoshaping and automaintenance.
http://www.uwm.edu/People/jcm/psy551/skinner.2/ho1

Observational Learning

Observational Learning—tutorial, basic, medium, links, graphics
Presents Bandura's original work on modeling with graphs.
http://www.valdosta.peachnet.edu/~whuitt/psy702/behsys/social.html

Observational Learning—tutorial, basic, short, links
Discusses observational learning in both animals and humans, gives an example of animal observational learning, and summarizes Bandura's original research.
http://www.science.wayne.edu/~wpoff/cor/mem/cognobsr.html

Social Learning Theory of Albert Bandura—text, adv., long, links
On–line chapter from a book provides in–depth overview of Bandura's theory of social learning. http://www.mhcollege.com/socscience/comm/bandur-s.mhtml

Observational Learning in Advertising—index, basic, short, links, graphics
The use of observational learning in advertising is illustrated through examples of advertisements. A link to an accompanying short paper explains the selection of the advertisements. http://www.calpoly.edu/~asbeug/ads/

Social Learning Among Mammals—text, interm., medium, links
A short summary of the 1996 winter meeting of the Primate Society of Great Britain (PSGB): papers, topics, and conclusions reached at the meeting. A link to the home page of the PSGB is provided.
http://www.ana.ed.ac.uk/PSGB/PrimateEye/61.WinterMeeting1996.html

Social Learning Key to Avian Harmony—article, interm., medium, links
Page from on–line version of the APA's *Monitor* (1996), article discusses recent research on the importance of social factors in bird behavior.
http://www.apa.org/monitor/nov96/birda.html

Studying Television Violence—article, adv., long, links, graphics
Very long but comprehensive article on television violence. Discusses history of the problem, paradigms of study, and expanding the agenda for research.
http://www.ksu.edu/humec/fshs/tv97.htm

Little Criminals—index, basic, short, links, graphics
Home page for the *Frontline* TV show (PBS), *Little Criminals,* has links to: questions and answers, interviews, and readings. The show was about juvenile violence and its relation to social learning.
http://www.pbs.org/wgbh/pages/frontline/shows/little/

Behavior Modification

PSI—index, interm., short, links
A page devoted to Personalized Student Instruction (PSI), includes links to essential components of PSI course, examples of such courses, references on PSI, and more. http://www.lafayette.edu/allanr/psi.html

Methods for Changing Behavior—tutorial, basic, long, links, graphics
Teaches people how to modify their own behavior: antecedent methods, during–the–behavior methods, and consequence methods.
http://www.cmhc.com/psyhelp/chap11/

Recovery Zone—index, interm., long, links
Home page for parents wishing to establish in–home ABA program (behavior modification) for their autistic children. Page includes numerous links to resources, testimonials, tax issues, and more.
http://pages.prodigy.com/dporcari/recovery_zone.html

Token TV—text, basic, medium, links, graphics
Commercial page for product, Token TV, that allows parents to provide tokens to their children that they may cash in for television viewing time.
http://www.midplains.net/~sstokes/

Chapter 7

Treatment for Phobias—text, basic, medium, links

Page provides a short description of behavioral treatment for phobias. Such treatment assumes that the phobia acquisition happened via classical conditioning. http://www.sonic.net/~fredd/treat.html

Writing Learning Objectives—tutorial, basic, medium, links, graphics

Provides instruction on how to write behavioral objectives in simple manner. Page includes overview, procedure, and examples.
http://cwis.usc.edu/hsc/med-sch/med-ed/object.html

Just for Fun

Oppatoons—graphic, basic, medium, links, graphics

Page features five cartoons of rats undergoing conditioning.
http://www.thecroft.com/psy/toons/OppaToons.html

Vegas Showgirls Slots—interactive, basic, short, links, graphics, Shockwave

From a commercial game site, slot machine that works on the Web, users may change their "wagers" and get "payoffs" while the program tallies the results. Good for demonstrating variable ratio schedules.
http://www.sabroco.com/greetings/WEB97/games/vegagame.htm

Memory

Memory is a topic of long standing in psychology. Ebbinghaus's original research began a long tradition of study in this field of psychology. Later, under the influence of events in computer technology, the information processing model was developed. Today, questions of how memory works, its physiology, and its reliability dominate. Resources in this chapter are arranged as follows: General Resources in Memory; Encoding; Storage; Retrieval and Forgetting; Physiology of Memory; Types of Memory Systems; Eyewitness Testimony and Repressed Memories; Improving Memory; and Just for Fun.

General Resources in Memory

Memory and Cognition Demonstrations and Tutorials—interactive, basic, short, links, graphics, Astound, Internet Explorer
A page of demonstrations in memory and cognition; requires Internet Explorer and Astound to use. Demonstrations are iconic memory, levels of processing, memory span, proactive interference, serial positions effect, and verbal rehearsal.
http://www.memcog.smsu.edu/

Tutorials and Demonstrations in Memory and Cognition—index, basic, short, links
This page collects 19 sites (some are interactive) in memory and cognition; including Stroop image, memory span, proactive interference, and more.
http://www.smsu.edu/contrib/psych/tutmem.html

Models of Memory—tutorial, interm., long, links, graphics
Tutorial on several models of memory: Atkinson–Shiffrin, levels of processing, Tulving's, and parallel distributed processing.
http://onesun.cc.geneseo.edu/~intd225/memmodls.html

Memory—tutorial, interm., long, links, graphics
Comprehensive overview of area of memory: Ebbinghaus, information processing model, basic research, short–term memory, longterm memory, encoding, storage, retrieval, forgetting, real world memory, studying, and more.
http://www.mindspring.com/~frudolph/lectures/Mem/memory.htm

Memory and Learning—index, basic, long, links, graphics
From the site Neuroscience for Kids, page has instructions for or links to demonstrations on memory and learning: What's Missing, Concentration, The Memory Game, There's a Chunk, Primacy–Recency Effect, Visualization, Acrostic It, The Space Place, and more.
http://weber.u.washington.edu/~chudler/chmemory.html

Papers on Memory in *Psychological Review* 1986–1987—biblio, adv., long, links
Lists papers written in the journal *Psychological Review* over the last ten years.
http://www.ntu.ac.uk/soc/bscpsych/memory/prevbib.htm

Human Capabilities—tutorial, interm., short, links, graphics
Tutorial from an engineering perspective on basic human capacities covers human senses, human memory, and human thought processes. http://www.cc.gatech.edu/classes/cs6751_97_winter/Topics/human-cap/intro.html

Papers in Memory—article, adv., medium, links, Acrobat
Six article abstracts whose full–text versions can be downloaded in Adobe Acrobat format. Topics include prospective and retrospective memory, Stroop effects, explicit and implicit memory, and more. http://gate.alfalab.ca/pgraf/paperidx.htm

The Information Processing Approach—tutorial, basic, long, links, graphics
Covers the basic issues of the information processing approach: general principles, stage model, alternative models, types of knowledge, and concept formation. Includes graphic of Atkinson–Shiffrin model, links to definitions, and hints for using information processing in the classroom. http://www.valdosta.peachnet.edu/~whuitt/psy702/cogsys/infoproc.html

Information Process Theory of Learning—tutorial, interm., long, links, graphics
Introduction to the information processing view: theorists, long–and short–term memory, factors affecting learning, and more. http://tiger.coe.missouri.edu/~t377/IPTheorists.html

Encoding

"The Magical Number Seven, Plus or Minus Two"—article, interm., long, links, graphics
The full text of George Miller's article (1956) "The Magical Number Seven, Plus or Minus Two: Some Limits on Our Capacity for Processing Information." This is a must read for any serious student of psychology. http://www.well.com/user/smalin/miller.html

Sensory Memory—tutorial, interm., medium, links, graphics
Discusses iconic and echoic memory. http://www.geneseo.edu/~intd225/sensmem.html

Short Term Memory—tutorial, interm., medium, links, graphics
Discusses methodology for studying STM, size of STM, and codes. http://www.geneseo.edu/~intd225/shorterm.html

Short Term Memory Demonstration—interactive, basic, short, links
Simple demonstration of the effect of stimulus length on short–term memory. http://pantheon.cis.yale.edu/~bayern/feb15-demo1.html

Short Term Memory Test—interactive, basic, short, links
Another demonstration of the relationship between stimulus length and short–term memory. http://weber.u.washington.edu/~chudler/stm0.html

Interactive Memory Quiz—interactive, basic, short, links, graphics, Shockwave
On–line memory quiz adapted by Daniel Schacter for the Web; displays three lists sequentially and then asks whether words presented were on any of the first three lists. Tests concept formation and context effects on memory. http://www.msnbc.com/onair/nbc/nightlynews/memory/default.asp

Imagery—tutorial, interm., long, links, graphics
Various aspects and theories of imagery are covered. Topics include theoretical controversy, analog theory, computational theory, characteristics of images, and Kosslyn's structural theory of imagery.
http://www.geneseo.edu/~intd225/imagery.html

The Art of Remembering—graphic, basic, short, links, graphics, RealAudio
An artist's memory is gauged by a painting he made of his home town and a recent photograph. Users may listen to a discussion as well.
http://www.exploratorium.edu/learning_studio/news/april97/mainstory5_apr97.html

Storage

How Many Bytes in Human Memory—article, interm., medium, links
Full–text article by Merkle (1988) about the size of human memory. Links lead to similar articles by others. http://www.merkle.com/humanMemory.html

Long Term Memory—tutorial, interm., long, links, graphics
Covers in detail: long–term or semantic memory and organization of semantic memory. http://www.geneseo.edu/~intd225/longterm.html

Retrieval and Forgetting

Tip of the Tongue—text, basic, medium, links
Describes the phenomenon and discusses research on the topic by Dahlgren.
http://www.indiana.edu/~rugs/rca/v17n1/24sb.html

State Dependent Memory—tutorial, basic, short, links
Discusses the phenomenon of state dependent memory. Sections are drugs, mood, moderators, and references.
http://ego.psy.flinders.edu.au/webpages/learning/kmtvbp/page1.html

"War of the Ghosts"—text, basic, short
Text of Bartlett's (1932) story used to test how memories were reconstructed. Shows the importance of deep structure on memory; the meaning of the story was remembered but the story was not remembered verbatim.
http://penta.ufrgs.br/edu/telelab/2/war-of-t.htm

Source Monitoring—graphic, adv., short, links, graphics
Describes source monitoring, or how people remember or fail to remember where they first learned an item. Includes a description of software for use in studying the phenomenon. http://xhuoffice.psyc.memphis.edu/gpt/talk/st/soudgm.htm

Common Cents— interactive, basic, short, links, graphics
Page shows Nickerson and Adams's (1979) famous demonstration of memory for a common object, a penny, click on the penny you think actually looks like one.
http://www.exploratorium.edu/memory/index.html

Theories of Forgetting—tutorial, interm., long, links, graphics
Covers the following theories of forgetting: decay, consolidation, interference, retrieval failure, and repression.
http://www.mtsu.edu/~sschmidt/Cognitive/forgetting/forgetting.html

Physiology of Memory

Memories Are Made of...—article, basic, medium, links, graphics
Article from *Scientific American* discusses the use of memory–enhancing drugs in Alzheimer's patients. http://www.sciam.com/0397issue/0397techbus1.html

Prefrontal Cortex and Working Memory—graphic, basic, short, links, graphics
Two color graphics of human and monkey brains showing area involved in working memory. http://www.sciam.com/0897issue/0897trendsbox1.htm

The Machinery of Thought—article, basic, long, links, graphics
Article from *Scientific American* describes recent research in the physiology of memory. Links in article lead to further information (i.e., nMRI, PET, and researchers). http://www.sciam.com/0896issue/temp/0897trends.html

fMRI Reveals Dynamics of Working Memory—article, basic, medium, links
Describes research using functional MRI technique where subjects are monitored as they perform cognitive tasks. The studies reveal a new and different picture of the physiology of working memory. http://www.nimh.nih.gov/events/prfmri.htm

Active Brain Areas in Working Memory—graphic, basic, short, graphics
Three–dimensional MRI reconstruction of subject's brain while holding a series of letters in working memory. Some parietal and frontal areas are active. http://www.nimh.nih.gov/events/prfmri2.htm

Amnesia—text, basic, short, links, graphics
Provides a basic definition of amnesia; discusses causes and prognoses. http://www.med.umich.edu/1libr/mental/amnes01.htm

Overview of Amnesia—tutorial, basic, short, links, graphics
From a page for medical students; covers retrograde and anterograde amnesia, differential diagnosis, and physiology. Links are provided for deeper exploration. http://www.medinfo.ufl.edu/year2/neuro/v1161.html

Amnesia Victim Gets Memory and Lost Assets Back—article, basic, medium, links, graphics
True story of an amnesia victim and how he regained his memory and his identity. http://www.ifast.com/true2.html

Types of Memory Systems

Mathematical Models of Human Memory—tutorial, adv., short, links
Page serves as an index for four tutorials in memory: theory of distributed associative memory, search of associative memory, the matrix model, and the list strength effect. The page also has links to three simulations: the SAM simulator, a MATRIX model simulator, and a TODAM simulator. http://psy.uq.edu.au/CogPsych/Noetica/OpenForumIssue6/introduction.html

Endel Tulving—index, interm., medium, links, graphics
Biography of prominent researcher in memory; includes personal and professional information, a story describing his classroom style, and links to related information. http://fas.sfu.ca/css/gcs/scientists/Tulving/tulving.html

Eyewitness Testimony and Repressed Memories

Eyewitness Memory—index, basic, medium, links
Some issues and highlights in the area of eyewitness memory are provided as links on this page.
http://www.wooster.edu/psychology/gillund/eyewitness/p340conn.html

Mona—interactive, basic, short, links, graphics, MPEG
Users may look at still or motion versions (in MPEG format) of Leonardo's masterpiece, the *Mona Lisa*. Something is wrong with Mona that can only be seen upright. http://www.exploratorium.edu/exhibits/mona/mona.html

Facial Analysis—index, interm., long, links, graphics
Links to 41 sites on facial analysis. http://mambo.ucsc.edu/psl/fanl.html

Repressed and Recovered Memories—index, interm., medium, links
Comprehensive site on the controversy of repressed and recovered memories. Provides links to both sides of the controversy.
http://www.ntu.ac.uk/soc/bscpsych/context/recover.htm

Questions and Answers about Memories of Childhood Abuse—text, basic, medium, links
From APA, a summary of the repressed memory issue in Q & A format.
http://www.apa.org/pubinfo/mem.html

Voices of Children—article, adv., long, links
Review of the book *Jeopardy in the Courtroom in Contemporary Psychology*. Discusses the issue of the veracity of children's testimony in courtrooms. http://www.apa.org/journals/cnt/jan97/ceci.html

Recovered Memories of Sexual Abuse—index, interm., long, links, graphics
This site argues for the existence and commonness of repressed memory and presents data to support that position. http://www.jimhopper.com/memory

Accused—index, basic, short, links, graphics, VDO
A private investigator and a lawyer have put these pages together as a service for clients accused of crimes via repressed testimony. The site includes streaming videos, documents on sexual crimes, documents on false memory, and more. http://www.accused.com/contents/

Doors of Memory—article, basic, long, links, graphics
Full–text article from *Mother Jones* (1993) on repressed memories, details one case from Texas. http://www.mojones.com/mother_jones/JF93/watters.html

Children in the Courtroom—index, basic, medium, links
This site provides links to specific cases, people involved in childhood testimony and repressed memory activities, and other related sites.
http://www.psych.nwu.edu/psych/people/grad/lampinen/A01SITES.html

False Memory Syndrome—index, interm., short, links, search
Home page of a group founded to combat the spread of false memory syndrome, site includes links to: false memory syndrome (definition), mailing lists, Internet resources, FAQ, and others. http://advicom.net/~fitz/fmsf/

Remembering Dangerously—article, interm., long, links, graphics, search
On–line version of *Skeptical Inquirer* (March, 1995) article by Elizabeth Loftus.
http://advicom.net/~fitz/csicop/si/9503/memory.html

The Myth of Repressed Memory—book, basic, long
Excerpt from book (one chapter) of same title in *Cosmopolitan,* the story of Eileen
Franklin and her memories.
http://weber.u.washington.edu/~eloftus/Articles/Cosmo.html

Improving Memory

Memory Techniques and Mnemonics—index, basic, short, links, graphics
Page provides links to information on mnemonics: introduction to memory
techniques, memory techniques explained, and applications of memory techniques.
http://www.demon.co.uk/mindtool/memory.html

SQ3R—tutorial, basic, medium, links
Users can learn how to improve their studying through the SQ3R (survey, question,
read, recite, and review) method.
http://www.gac.peachnet.edu/student_affairs/study_skills/effstdy.html

Distributing Practice Over Time—text, basic, short, links
Discusses the studying strategy of distributed practice and how it produces better
results than massed practice. http://www.nprdc.navy.mil/wworks/find6.htm

Tips on Taking Multiple Choice Tests—tutorial, basic, long, links
Provides tips for successful test taking on multiple choice tests. Tips: simulate the
required behavior, pace yourself, don't skip around, and many more.
http://www.wesleyan.edu/spn/testtips.htm

Just for Fun

False Memory Test—interactive, basic, medium, links, graphics
Provides a list of words to read to "subjects" and target words to test with
afterwards. Users should be able to cause false memories reliably using both.
Article provides an explanation of the effect.
http://www.sciam.com/0597issue/0597scicit3.html

Pavlov's Memory Enhancer—interactive, basic, short, links, graphics Shockwave
Slick commercial on–line software that simulates Sperling's partial report
procedure. http://www.sabroco.com/greetings/WEB97/games/pav_game.htm

Language and Cognition

Language and cognition are two intertwined areas in psychology. Much research is done in both of those areas, and much of that research is conducted in areas outside of psychology. Ironically, that interdisciplinary competition often leads to an inability to communicate between scientists from different disciplines even though they work in very similar subject areas. Cognitive science and artificial intelligence are two new areas related to cognition. Below, Web resources are organized in the following areas: Animal Communication; Language; Problem Solving; Decisions and Errors in Cognition; Cognitive Science and Artificial Intelligence; and Just for Fun.

Animal Communication

Language in Apes—tutorial, basic, long, links, graphics
Covers many of the aspects of research on ape language: how apes communicate in the wild, history of the apes and language question, Washoe, Sarah, Lana, Nim, dichotomy in the scientific community, and more.
http://math.uwaterloo.ca/~dmswitze/apelang.html

The Question of Primate Language—article, basic, long, links, graphics
From the National Zoo, this article covers basic issues in primate communication and intelligence. http://www.fonz.org/main.htm

Communication with Parrots—index, basic, short, links, graphics
Page contains information and links about Pepperberg's research with Alex and other African grey parrots. http://www.cages.org/research/pepperberg/index.html

Crocodilian Communication—audio, interm., short, links, graphics
Page provides audio files of calls of different species of crocodilians and speculates as to the nature of those sounds in inter- and intraspecific communication.
http://www.flmnh.ufl.edu/natsci/herpetology/brittoncrocs/croccomm.html

Language

The Psychology of Language—index, interm., long, links
Comprehensive page on language includes links to researchers, labs and programs, organizations, meetings, journals, books, software, and more.
http://www.psyc.memphis.edu/POL/POL.htm

Linguistics—tutorial, interm., long, links, graphics
Comprehensive look at language issues: Hockett's 13 design features of language, grammatical theory and language structure, phase structure grammars, Chomsky's transformational grammar, and evidence for innate origins.
http://www.geneseo.edu/~intd225/linguist.html

Human Language Functions—tutorial, basic, medium, links
Discusses topics on language: language is more than communication, interpersonal communication, language within the individual, and language and society.
http://wilmot.unh.edu/~jel/Lfunctions.html

Human Language Systems—index, adv., long, links
Provides links to 26 ongoing projects in language systems sponsored by DARPA.
http://www.darpa.mil/ito/research/hls/index.html

Phonetics—index, interm., medium, links, graphics
Provides links to FAQs, demos, and other miscellaneous sites in phonetics. Sites featuring voice synthesis, signal processing, and others are included.
http://www.ims.uni-stuttgart.de/phonetik/joerg/worldwide/FAQs.html

sci.lang FAQ—FAQ, basic, long, links
This FAQ answers 23 questions about linguistics. Site contains questions about prehistoric language, Chomsky, Creoles, and more.
http://www.tezcat.com/~markrose/langfaq.html

Meta Index of Linguistics Resources—index, basic, long, links
Comprehensive index of sites in linguistics categories include linguistic theories, linguistic conferences, linguistic journals, companies, and more.
http://www.sultry.arts.su.edu.au/links/linguistics.html

Metaphors—tutorial, basic, short
A page describing the basics of metaphors.
http://www.desk.nl/~acsi/WS/themes/metacc1.htm

Center for the Cognitive Science of Metaphor—index, basic, medium, links
A comprehensive page of links on metaphors.
http://metaphor.uoregon.edu/metaphor.htm

Conceptual Metaphor Home Page—index, basic, short, links
A page that lists metaphors via three indeces: metaphor name, source domain, and target domain. Users may look up metaphors through those indeces.
http://cogsci.berkeley.edu/

The Uses of Baby Talk—article, interm., long, links
The effects of "motherese," or how adults alter their voice, intonation, and pitch to communicate with infants, is described and discussed.
http://ericps.ed.uiuc.edu/npin/respar/texts/fampeer/usetalk.html

What Does Your Baby Hear?—text, basic, short, links, graphics
Page describes typical basic hearing competencies of infants and children and lists when in life those competencies normally develop.
http://www.sunshinecottage.org/babyhear.html

Language Development—tutorial, basic, long, links
Covers most aspects of early language development including definition of language, comprehension vs. production, theories of language, and others.
http://www.cee.umn.edu/dis/courses/CPSY1301_8283_02.www/course/06.html

Language Topics—index, basic, medium, links
   A long list of lecture outlines (33) in language, including concepts from linguistics, concepts from cognitive psychology, word meaning, speech sounds, stages of acquisition, and more.
   http://web.psych.ualberta.ca/~pdixon/357/96-97%20Lectures.html

Language Arts and Children's Literature Test—interactive, basic, short, links
   Test on basic information in language arts and children's literature; provides instant feedback via pull–down answers.
   http://www.ed.wright.edu/cehs/mgifford/test1.htm

Phonetics—tutorial, interm., short, links, graphics
   Covers the basics of phonetics, the study of sound formation in language: speech errors, consonant and vowel articulation, phonemes, and more. Includes spectrograms of sounds.
   http://lx.cog.brown.edu/courses/cg22/wk02/phonetics.html

Grammar and Style Notes—tutorial, basic, medium, links, search
   A guide to grammar and style for English by a teacher; also includes references and links to other on–line resources.
   http://www.english.upenn.edu/~jlynch/Grammar/

Noam Chomsky—text, basic, short, graphics
   Provides photo, basic biography, list of major publications, and some quotes.
   http://www.worldmedia.com/manucon/cards/chomsky.htm

Skinner's Approach to Verbal Behavior—text, adv., long
   Describes Skinner's approach to language in detail.
   http://www.uwm.edu/People/jcm/psy551/skinner.2/ho4

Language and Thought—text, interm., medium, links
   Discusses the relationship of thought and language: linguistic relativity vs. linguistic determinism, and investigating language and thought.
   http://www.lsadc.org/Slobin.html

Concepts—tutorial, adv., long, links
   Discusses properties of concepts, provides example of concept (i.e., "harp"). Sections include ways of thinking about concepts, why do concepts matter, basic categories, networks and hierarchies, conceptual complexity, and others.
   http://alan.lrdc.pitt.edu/psych5/lec5.htm

Oakland School District Synopsis of the Adopted Policy on Standard American English Language Development—text, adv., long, links
   Linked version of the controversial policy adopted by the Oakland school district.
   http://www.ousd.k12.ca.us/oakland.standard.html

On–line Guide to Gang Signs and Grafitti—tutorial, interm., short, links, graphics
   Two part guide to gang signs and to gang grafitti.
   http://www.courses.edu/gang-guide.html

Sounds of the World's Animals—index, basic, short, links, graphics
   Page provides links to how speakers of different languages say common sounds that animals make. http://www.georgetown.edu/cball/animals/animals.html

Vocabulary Tests—index, basic, short, links, graphics
Users may take or download short tests of adult vocabulary.
http://www.educ.goteborg.se/usam/pforum/elpa/bin/nsvt001a.doc

Problem Solving

Problem Solving and Analytical Techniques—index, basic, short, links, graphics
Page links to several methods of problem solving: brainstorming, critical path
analysis, decision trees, force field analysis, PMI, and SWOT analysis.
http://www.mindtools.com/page2.html

Problem Solving—tutorial, interm., long, links, graphics
Covers many aspects of problem solving: types of problems, types of solutions,
classic terms, and others.
http://www.mtsu.edu/~sschmidt/Cognitive/Problem/problem.html

Breaking the Mental Set—tutorial, basic, long, links, graphics
Teaches about mental set and how to overcome its effects. Includes many
problems (with solutions) to illustrate mental set.
http://www.andrew.cmu.edu/user/landau/mental_set.html

Critical Thinking—index, basic, medium, links, graphics
Information on the heuristics of problem solving and a few problems to solve.
http://www.beth.k12.pa.us/schools/broughal/rivera/critical_thinking.html

An Application Oriented Tutorial on Heuristics—index, adv., short, links,
graphics
Tutorial covers topics in problem solving heuristics: heuristic problem solving,
genetic algorithms, neural networks, evaluating heuristics, np completeness, and
other topics. http://mat.gsia.cmu.edu/applic/notes/node18.html

Concept–based Problem Solving in Physics—article, adv., long, links, graphics
Discusses the use of concept–based problem solving in the teaching of physics.
Paper has useful tables listing types of knowledge needed to solve problems and
mental processes that help students develop their problem solving skills (links on
page). http://www-perg.phast.umass.edu/UMPERG/papers/CBPSP/CBPSP.html

Metacognition—text, basic, short, links
Defines metacognition and lists characteristics of metacognition before, during, and
after an action.
http://www.ncrel.org/skrs/areas/issues/students/learning/lr1metn.htm

Expert Chess Memory—abstract, interm., short
Abstract of Gobet and Simon's (1996) article on chunking in chess; they confirmed
earlier work by Chase and Simon (1973).
http://psyc.nott.ac.uk/aigr/people/frg/chunk-experiment-abstract.html

The Psychology of Invention—index, interm., short, links, graphics
Site is dedicated to exploring how invention and discovery happen, including links
to: To Fly is Everything, The Circle of Thought, Invention of the Telephone,
Psychology of Science, The Invention Dimension, and a bibliography.
http://hawaii.cogsci.uiuc.edu/invent/invention.html

Calvin and Hobbes Game—interactive, basic, short, links, graphics
A version of the missionaries and cannibals (or Hobbits and Orcs) problem that users can play on–line.
http://www.psych.nwu.edu/psych/people/resappt/yamada/ch-game.html

The Wason Selection Task—interactive, basic, short, links, graphics
Page begins with the abstract version of the task (solved at first try by less than 10% of college students) and has a link to the concrete version of the task (solved at first try by more than 70% of college students). The logical rule for both is: if p then q, and if not p then not q.
http://pangaea.pratt.edu/~jlampin/wason.html

Three Door Problem—interactive, basic, medium, links, graphics, ActiveX, Internet Explorer
Can you make the right decision when you fail to get the prize after your first choice? Should you switch or stay with your original choice?
http://www.iotasys.com/think/3doors/

Three Door Problem—interactive, basic, medium, links, graphics
This version works with any late–model browser. Can you make the right decision when you fail to get the prize after your first choice. Should you switch or stay with your original choice? http://www.iotasys.com/think/3d_cgi/index.htm

Tower of Hanoi—interactive, basic, short, links, graphics, Java
A version of the tower of Hanoi puzzle that users may play on–line; users may reset the initial number of rings.
http://www.tenthhouse.com/funpages/hanoi/

Four Brain Teasers—interactive, basic, short, links, graphics
Page links to four problems to test your problem solving abilities; answers are provided. http://www.bankerstrust.com/hr/games/teaser1.html

Three Men and a Hotel—interactive, basic, short, links, graphics
Users may try to solve this classic logic problem. Answer is provided.
http://weber.u.washington.edu/~jlks/hotel.html

The Pattern Game—interactive, basic, short, links, graphics
A problem to solve using letters. Remember your problem solving set examples. Answer is provided.
http://weber.u.washington.edu/~jlks/pattern.html

Decisions and Errors in Cognition

Amos Tversky—text, basic, medium
Obituary of Amos Tversky, famous for his research in decision making and risk assessment. http://rowlf.cc.wwu.edu:8080/~market/tj/tversky.html

Decision Making—tutorial, adv., long, links
Covers prescriptive models of decision making, evidence for irrational decision making, descriptive models of decision making, bounded rationality, representativeness heuristic, availability heuristic, and others.
http://penta.ufrgs.br/edu/telelab/2/lec10.htm

Making Decisions—tutorial, interm., short, links
Another tutorial on decision making, topics cover: features of a decision, three main heuristics, personality of decision makers, and more.
http://www.aston.ac.uk/~golderpa/CS342/notes/Dss1.htm

Cognitive Science and Artificial Intelligence

Cognitive Science Dictionary—index, basic, short, links
Defines 73 terms in cognitive science.
http://penta.ufrgs.br/edu/telelab/3/control.htm

Celebrities in Cognitive Science—index, basic, medium, links
Page has biographic information on researchers in cognitive science. People linked are: Phil Agre, Jay David Bolter, Vannevar Bush, John Carroll, Noam Chomsky, William Clancey, Edward deBono, Hubert Dreyfus, Stevan Harnad, Douglas Hofstadter, Kevin Kelly, George Landow, Brenda Laurel, Marvin Minsky, Donald Norman, Seymore Papert, Howard Rheingold, Roger Schank, John Searle, Herbert Simon, Sherry Turkle, Terry Winograd, Etienne Wenger, and Lev Vygotsky. The page also links to six similar sites.
http://www.cudenver.edu/~mryder/itc_data/cogsci.html

Norbert Wiener—text, interm., medium, links
A memoir and short biography of Norbert Wiener, founder of cybernetics and early pioneer in cognitive science.
http://ic.www.media.mit.edu/JBW/ARTICLES/WIENER/WIENER1.HTM

Claude Shannon—index, basic, short, links, graphics
Page from AT&T contains a short biography of Claude Shannon, whose 1948 paper on information theory serves as basis for much of modern psychology and cognitive science. The full text of that paper is available as a link from the page.
http://www.att.com/attlabs/archive/shannon.html

John von Neumann—index, interm., short, links, graphics
Simple page that contains several links to biographical information on John von Neumann and to some of his original papers. Neumann was instrumental in developing the modern computer.
http://nano.xerox.com/nanotech/vonNeumann.html

Computers: From the Past to the Present—tutorial, interm., medium, links, graphics
Comprehensive look at computers and computation from prehistoric time until the present. Topics include: the difference engine, Alan Turing, the creation of Microsoft, the Web, and more.
http://www.ifi.unizh.ch/groups/se/people/hoyle/Lecture/

Obsolete Computer Museum—index, basic, medium, links, graphics
A page dedicated to not so old but very obsolete computers. Brands include: Amstrad, Apple, Atari, Commodore, Epson, IBM, NEC, Osborne, Sinclair, Tandy, and many others.
http://www.ncsc.dni.us/fun/user/tcc/cmuseum/cmuseum.htm

Information Age—index, basic, medium, links, graphics
Page illustrates artifacts in information technology from an exhibit at the National Museum of American History: the Morse telegraph, telephones, a stock ticker, Hollerith tabulating machine, the Enigma machine (decoder used in World War II), and more. http://photo2.si.edu/infoage.html

A Brief History of the Internet—text, interm., long, links
A highly linked page that tells the story of the Internet written by those who helped create the global communications network.
http://www.isoc.org/internet-history/

Artificial Intelligence—tutorial, interm., long, links, graphics
Comprehensive review of AI, covers: modern theoretical antecedents, first successes in AI, microworlds, expert systems, and frames and scripts.
http://www.geneseo.edu/~intd225/artint.html

AI on the Web—index, interm., long, links
Very comprehensive site (680 links) on artificial intelligence (AI), organized like the book, *AI: A Modern Approach.* Topics are overview of AI, intelligent agents, search and game playing, logic and knowledge representation, planning, reasoning with uncertainty, machine learning, natural language processing, perception and robotics, philosophy and the future, and AI programming. Links to other AI sites also.
http://http.cs.berkeley.edu/~russell/ai.html

Dawson's Margin Notes on Vehicles—index, interm., medium, links, graphics
Provides links keyed to Valentino Braitenberg's book, *Vehicles,* seminal in the area of synthetic psychology, or psychology from the bottom up. The vehicles are mechanistic thought experiments whose "physiology" is known, making their behavior more easily explainable.
http://web.psych.ualberta.ca/~mike/Pearl_Street/Vehicles/home.html

Braitenberg Vehicles—index, basic, medium, links, graphics
Page with links to QuickTime and MPEG movies of vehicle simulations. Also has links to other pages on vehicles.
http://www.cs.uchicago.edu/~wiseman/vehicles/

Everyone's Guide to DNA Computers—index, basic, long, links, graphics
Users can explore the latest experimental technology in computer design, DNA. Page has links to student and scientific levels of information.
http://www.clearlight.com/~morph/dna/dne.htm

Visual Interface Design—tutorial, interm., short, links, graphics
Teaches about the design principles behind effective computer interfaces: defining VID, the art of design, the rules of the screen, layout, how to do VID, and the future of user interfaces.
http://www.quidnunc.com/knowledge/vid/vid.html

Artificial Intelligence Methods—tutorial, interm., medium, links, graphics
Course on AI covers philosophy, search, game playing, knowledge representation, expert systems, machine learning, and neural networks.
http://tawny.cs.nott.ac.uk/~sbx/winnie/aim/topics.htm

Just for Fun

Model Languages—index, adv., short, links, graphics
All anyone would ever want to know about model languages (i.e., Esperanto, Klingon, Elvish, etc.). Includes a FAQ.
http://members.aol.com/JAHenning/homepage.htm

Totally Twisted Grammar—index, basic, short, links
Page contains links to a variety of sites that poke fun at language (intentionally or unintentionally). Links include a glossary of hardboiled slang, dictionary of street drug slang, Britishisms, Klingon, and more.
http://www.english.uiuc.edu/english302/twisted.htm

Save the Adverb—index, basic, short, links, graphics
Home page of an attempt to halt and reverse the adverb's demise.
http://www.cs.wisc.edu/~dgarrett/adverb/

Eliza—interactive, basic, short
Provides an on–line version of the famous program where a computer attempts to simulate a human interacting with a user.
http://www-ai.ijs.si/eliza/eliza.html

MovieLens—interactive, basic, short, links
Page uses collaborative filtering to choose movies for users after they answer questions about their own movie preferences. The page will then make movie suggestions based on an analysis of similar patterns by other respondents.
http://www.movielens.umn.edu/

Intelligence and Testing

Since Binet was first asked to create a method of screening children prior to their entering school, the psychology of testing and intelligence have come a long way. Today, tests have become commonplace and are a big business. Still, the basic science behind intelligence remains elusive and controversial. The nature–nurture issue is alive and well here, as evidence about the contributions to intelligence from the genome and from the environment remain basically unexplained. Intelligence itself is not easily defined nor studied. Despite those problems, much is known and more is practiced today in the area of intelligence and testing than in the past. A related area, creativity is also included. The resources in this chapter are arranged as follows: General Resources in Intelligence and Testing; Basic Principles; History; Characteristics of Tests; Extremes; Heredity and Environment; New Methods; Creativity; and Just for Fun.

General Resources in Intelligence and Testing

FAQ on Psychological Tests—text, interm., long
From APA, lists and answers commonly asked questions about tests and testing.
http://www.apa.org/science/test.html

ERIC Clearinghouse on Assessment and Evaluation—index, basic, short, links, graphics, search
Comprehensive site on testing and assessment; links to many resources: search ERIC, test locator, assessment FAQs, and a full–text library. Many other links point to related resources. http://ericae.net/

Buros Institute of Mental Measures—index, basic, short, links
The home page of one of the major sources of tests, with links to test locators, test reviews, fax services, *Mental Measurements Yearbook, Tests in Print,* and to other related resources. http://www.unl.edu/buros/

Psychometric Testing—index, basic, short, links, graphics
From the Mind Tools pages, links to: Discover your Learning Style, IQ test, Myers–Briggs Personality Test, and VALS/Life Style Survey.
http://www.mindtools.com/page12.html

Keirsey Temperament Sorter—index, basic, medium, links
Home page of the test derived from Jungian personality theory; provides links to information about the test and to on–line versions of the test in four languages.
http://keirsey.com/

ACT Home—index, basic, short, links, graphics
  The home page of the American College Testing Service (ACT) provides links to ACT assessment, work keys, ACT news, and more. http://www.act.org/

College Board Online—index, basic, short, links, graphics, search
  The home page of the College Board (SAT test), provides links to news, test dates, on–line registration, college search, and more. http://www.collegeboard.org/

ETSnet—index, basic, short, links, graphics, search
  The home page of the Educational Testing Service (ETS), creators of tests such as the AP series, TOEFL, SAT, GRE, and others. http://www.ets.org/

100 Most Common SAT Words—tutorial, basic, long, links
  From a purveyor of test preparation materials, an analysis of the words most likely to help students on the SAT. http://www.kaplan.com/precoll/sat_words.html

GRE OnLine—index, basic, short, links, graphics, search
  The home page of the Graduate Record Exam (GRE) provides links to sample test questions, free publications, news, and more. http://www.gre.org/

MBA Explorer—index, basic, short, links, graphics
  The home page of the Graduate Management Admission Test (GMAT) provides links to GMAT information, MBA facts and fiction, financing your MBA, and more. http://www.gmat.org/index.htm

LSAC Online—index, basic, short, links, graphics
  The home page of the Law School Admission Council provides links to events, information; and to Reggie (a tool for admission), and other related services. http://www.lsac.org/

Miller Analogies Test—index, basic, short, links, graphics
  The home page of the Miller Analogies Test provides a sample question and telephone number where to get additional information. http://www.hbtpc.com/mat/

Psychological Tests and Resources—index, interm., short, links
  Links to tests, literature searches, analyses, and other aspects of testing. http://www.wp.com/mehrab/home.html

Tools—tutorial, basic, medium, links, graphics
  Short descriptions of some commonly used tests: Bender (Bender Visual Motor Gestalt Test), Conners Parent Rating Scale, DAP (Draw–a–Person Test), Kinetic Family Drawing, MAT (Matrix Analogies Test), Reynolds (Revised Children's Manifest Anxiety Scale), TAT (Thematic Apperception Test), Vineland Adaptive Behaviour Scales, and WISC–III (Wechsler Intelligence Scale for Children–III). http://www.pangea.ca/~mwady/tests1.html

Basic Principles

Definition—text, basic, short, links, graphics
  A short definition of a psychological test. http://www.sbs.org.uk/sbs/what.htm

Reliability and Validity Quiz—interactive, interm., long, links
  Page asks 11 matching questions about types of reliability and validity. Answers are provided. http://www.selu.edu/Academics/Education/EDF600/cw7d.htm

Layman's Guide to Social Research Methods—index, basic, short, links, graphics
Page contains links to tutorials: reliability and validity, strengthening your analysis, glossary, and other related sites.
http://trochim.human.cornell.edu/tutorial/Colosi/lcolosi1.htm

Questionnaire Design—tutorial, basic, long, links, graphics
Covers issues in questionnaire design: defining objectives of survey, writing the questionnaire, now what, and others.
http://www.cc.gatech.edu/classes/cs6751_97_winter/Topics/quest-design/

Basic Principles in Testing—index, basic, short, links, graphics
From the Oncology Nursing Certification Corporation, links to eight tutorial articles on testing including item writing, test item analysis, test validity and reliability, scoring, and others.
http://www.oncc.org/pages/special_publications/specpub_toc.htm

History

Sir Francis Galton—text, basic, short, links
Short biography of Galton, early pioneer in the testing of human abilities.
http://userwww.sfsu.edu/~rsauzier/Galton.html

Alfred Binet—text, basic, short, links
Short biography of Binet, the developer of the first intelligence test.
http://userwww.sfsu.edu/~rsauzier/Binet.html

The Philosophy of Intelligence—tutorial, interm., long, links
Discusses topics in the history of testing: Binet and global intelligence, Terman's IQ formula and the Stanford–Binet, Spearman's two–factor theory, Thurstone and primary mental abilities, the Wechsler compromise, and others.
http://www.psych.ucalgary.ca/CourseNotes/PSYC331/StudyTools/StudentContributions/DRobbins.html

Where Have All of the Women Gone?—tutorial, interm., long, links
Discusses the contributions of three women pioneers to testing: Mary Whiton Calkins, Margaret Floy Washburn, and Christine Ladd–Franklin.
http://www.psych.ucalgary.ca/CourseNotes/PSYC331/StudyTools/StudentContributions/harrington.html

The Structure of Success—article, adv., long, links, graphics
First of Richard Lemann's articles (1995) in *The Atlantic* on the history of ETS (Educational Testing Service).
http://www.theatlantic.com/issues/95sep/ets/grtsort1.htm

The Great Sorting—article, adv., long, links, graphics
Second of Richard Lemann's articles (1995) in *The Atlantic* on the history of the ETS (Educational Testing Service).
http://www.theatlantic.com/issues/95sep/ets/grtsort2.htm

Characteristics of Tests

The Knowns and Unknowns of Intelligence—text, basic, short, links, graphics, search
From APA, lists and discusses known and unknown characteristics of intelligence and intelligence tests. http://www.apa.org/releases/intell.html

Be Careful of How You Define Intelligence—article, basic, short, links, search
Robert J. Sternberg discusses cross–cultural differences in intelligence. He concludes, " We can't assume that the cognitive skills we value or label as intelligence are those valued or labeled in another culture." http://www.apa.org/monitor/oct97/define.html

The Standard Normal Distribution—tutorial, basic, short, links, graphics
Provides basic definition of normal curve and shows areas under the curve. http://www.ruf.rice.edu/~lane/hyperstat/A75494.html

Are Today's IQ Tests Really Better Than Those of Yesterday?—text, basic, short, links
Discussion of modern IQ tests compared to traditional ones. Concludes that major improvements are technical not psychometric or multicultural. http://www.naspweb.org/office/spr/IE262.HTM

Which Traits Predict Job Perfomance—article, basic, medium, links, graphics
From APA's *Monitor,* article (1995) discusses factors associated in predicting job success from other measurable dimensions. http://www.apa.org/monitor/jul95/personal.html

Tests, Tests, Tests—index, basic, long, links, graphics
Page links to personality tests, intelligence tests, and attitude, lifestyle and emotional tests. Page also has links to other related sites. http://www.queendom.com/tests.html

Extremes

AAMR—index, basic, long, links, graphics
Home page of the American Association on Mental Retardation (AAMR), has links to resources and services they provide. http://aamr.org/

The ARC—index, basic, long, links, graphics
Home page of The ARC, a national organization on mental retardation, the page contains many links to resources for those interested in or dealing with mental retardation. http://TheArc.org/welcome.html

Special Education Glossary of Terms—table, basic, long, links, graphics, search
A list of defined terms relevant to special education, disability, and retardation. http://specialed.miningco.com/

Introduction to Mental Retardation—FAQ, basic, long, links
Page provides questions and answers on basic questions about mental retardation. http://TheArc.org/faqs/mrqa.html

Genetic Causes of Mental Retardation—FAQ, basic, long, links
Page provides questions and answers to questions about the genetic causes of mental retardation. http://TheArc.org/faqs/mrqa.html

Bazelon Center for Mental Health Law—index, basic, short, links, graphics
Home page of a law group dealing with mental health, site has links to: publications, alerts and updates, managed care information, and more.
http://www.bazelon.org/

LD OnLine—index, basic, short, links, graphics, search
Comprehensive page is a service of the Learning Disabilities Project at WETA, provides links to: ABC's of LD/ADD, LD in depth, first person, and more.
http://www.ldonline.org/index.html

ADA Overview—text, basic, short, links
Provides a short outline of the major facets of the ADA laws.
http://janweb.icdi.wvu.edu/kinder/overview.htm

ADA Accessibility Guidelines—index, adv., long, links, graphics
The complete ADA guidelines. The site has 10 linked sections for easy searching.
http://www.access-board.gov/bfdg/adaag.htm

Gifted and Talented—index, basic, short, links, graphics
Page has sections on: fun stuff for kids, Internet links, articles, journals, magazines, books and other publications, schools, research, and miscellaneous.
http://205.121.65.141/Millville/Teachers/TAG/gifted2.htm

TAG Family Network—index, basic, short, links, graphics
Home page of the TAG Family Network, an organization "dedicated to appropriate education for talented and gifted youth, and advocacy." Page contains articles, links to other resources, and a membership form.
http://www.teleport.com/~rkaltwas/tag/index.html

IAAY—index, interm., short, links
Home page of the Institute for the Academic Advancement of Youth (IAAY), includes links to: history of their organization, Center for Talent Identification, research projects, and others. http://www.jhu.edu:80/~gifted/

A Short Summary of Giftedness—text, basic, medium, links
Provides definitional characteristics of giftedness and links to other resources on the topic. http://www.eskimo.com/%7Euser/zbrief.html

Helping Your Highly Gifted Child—article, basic, long, links
Advice for parents of gifted children, includes sections on: differences, public attitudes, school, lack of fit, and others.
http://www.kidsource.com/kidsource/content/help.gift.html

Gifted Students not Being Challenged Enough by U.S. School System—article, basic, medium, links, graphics, search
From APA, synopsis on article about new book, *Gifted Children: Myths and Realities* (1997) by Ellen Winner. Article argues that schools do not do enough for academically gifted students.
http://www.apa.org/releases/gifted.html

Heredity and Environment

Electronic Genetics Newsletter—index, basic, short, links, graphics
Page contains links to articles on interaction of genetics and behavior.
http://www.westpub.com/Educate/mathsci/cummmain.htm

Genetic Principle of Heritability—text, basic, short, links
Page explains the principle of heritability using dairy cows as an example, has link to table of heritable characteristics in dairy cows.
http://hammock.ifas.ufl.edu/txt/fairs/ds/2705.html

Genes and Behavior—index, interm., short, links, graphics, Java
Links to articles on genetics and behavior, articles cover: *The Bell Curve,* genes, environments and individual choice, from genomes to dreams, diversity and deviance, and our genes, ourselves (see immediately below). Page also has a forum link. http://serendip.brynmawr.edu/gen_beh/

Our Genes, Ourselves?—article, adv., long, links
From *BioScience,* article summarizes much of the research about gene–behavior interactions, criticizes twin studies, and discusses the problem of conducting research in human genetics.
http://serendip.brynmawr.edu/gen_beh/Berkowitz.html

Recent Developments in Human Behavioral Genetics—article, adv., long, links
From the *American Journal of Human Genetics* (1997), summarizes the current state of knowledge in human behavioral genetics.
http://www.faseb.org/genetics/ashg/policy/pol-28.htm

Two Views of the Bell Curve—article, adv., long, links, graphics, search
From *Contemporary Psychology,* two opposing views on the book *The Bell Curve* (1994), articles are: "Breaking the Last Taboo" and "Soft Science with a Neoconservative Agenda." http://www.apa.org/journals/bell.html

Robert Sternberg on the Bell Curve—article, interm., long, links
Skeptic magazine interview about Sternberg's views on the *Bell Curve* (1994).
http://www.skeptic.com/03.3.fm-sternberg-interview.html

The Bell Curve Flattened—article, adv., long, links, graphics, search
Nicholas Lemann summarizes methodological objections to the *Bell Curve* (1994).
http://www.slate.com/Features/BellCurve/BellCurve.asp

Stereotype Vulnerability: Effects on Test Performance—text, interm., short, links
Summarizes data on test performance and race and discusses its effects. Based on research done by Steele and Aronson (1995).
http://www.nsf.gov/sbe/srs/wmpdse94/chap5/sidebar4.htm

Upstream: Issues: Genetics—index, interm., short, links, graphics, search
Page contains eight articles on genetics and behavior. Articles include: ancient eugenics, eugenics and human nature, ideology and censorship in behavioral eugenics, and more.
http://www.cycad.com/cgi-bin/Upstream/Issues/genetics/index.html

Chinese Parents' Influence on Academic Performance—article, adv., long, links
   Literature review article (1995) on the relationship of culture and academic performance. http://www.ncbe.gwu.edu/miscpubs/nysabe/vol10/nysabe106.html

New Methods

Structure of Intellect—tutorial, basic, short, links, graphics
   Discusses Guilford's structure of intellect theory.
   http://www.gwu.edu/~tip/guilford.html

Triarchic Model for Teaching for Thinking—text, basic, short, links, graphics
   Provides basic information about Sternberg's triarchic (analytic, creative, and practical) model of intelligence.
   http://www.cyberspace.com/~building/trm_sternberg.html

Triarchic Theory—tutorial, basic, short, links, graphics
   Outlines the basic components and their relationships in Sternberg's triarchic theory. http://www.gwu.edu/~tip/stern.html

Howard Garner—index, basic, short, links, graphics
   Page contain links to information about Howard Gardner and his theory of multiple intelligences.
   http://www.ed.psu.edu/~ae-insys-wfed/INSYS/ESD/Gardner/menu.html

Interview: Howard Gardner—article, basic, long, links, graphics
   From CIO Magazine, Howard Gardner discusses his theory of multiple intelligences. http://www.cio.com/archive/031596_qa.html

Creativity

Odyssey of the Mind—index, basic, medium, links, graphics
   The home page for a national organization that sponsors creative problem solving contests. Page has links to: general information, associations, related links, and others. http://www.odyssey.org/

Creativity—tutorial, basic, short, links
   Provides a basic overview of creativity. http://www.gwu.edu/~tip/create.html

Creativity Web—index, basic, short, links, graphics
   Page has links to resources on creativity, including: creativity basics, children's corner, developing imagination, creative genius gallery, and more.
   http://www.ozemail.com.au/~caveman/Creative/

Just for Fun

Personality and IQ Tests—index, basic, short, links, graphics, Java
   Comprehensive site that provides links to personality tests and IQ tests that are scored automatically after users take them.
   http://www.davideck.com/online-tests.html

Uncommonly Diffficult IQ Tests—index, interm., long, links
   For users who want a challenge, a long list of "difficult" IQ tests.
   http://www.eskimo.com/~miyaguch/

Chapter 10

IQ Tests—index, basic, short, links, graphics
Provides links to a number of IQ tests and similar items. Has link to comments about answers.
http://www.stud.ntnu.no/studorg/mensa/iq.html

11

Motivation and Emotion

Motivation research attempts to answer psychology's "why" question. Many people are interested in knowing why people behave the way they do. Traditional answers center on hard–wired or on learned motives. Newer explanations invoke evolutionary and adaptive reasons for motivation. Closely related to motivation is emotion. Emotions are also largely hard–wired and are, in their own way, motivational. Both areas and their interrelationships are explored in this chapter. The resources in this chapter are arranged as follows: General Resources in Motivation and Emotion; Theories; Hunger and Thirst; Sexual Motives; Achievement; Emotional Experience; and Just for Fun.

General Resources in Motivation and Emotion

Evolutionary Psychology for the Common Person—index, basic, short, links, graphics
Introduces the field of evolutionary psychology and includes links to what is evolutionary psychology, essays and theories, and other related links.
http://www.evoyage.com/

Motivation—tutorial, basic, short, links, graphics
Covers basic topics in motivation: Maslow's hierarchy of needs, biological motivation, social and cognitive motivation, and others.
http://www.ed.ac.uk/~mlc/marble/psycho/topic2/topic2_c.htm

Motivation—text, basic, long, links, graphics
Discussion of data and theory of motivation from Mental Health Net; covers how to get motivated and the importance of setting goals.
http://www.cmhc.com/psyhelp/chap4/chap4i.htm

Increasing Your Motivation Level—tutorial, basic, short, links, graphics
Advice from a university learning center; discusses raising one's motivation via recognizing one's locus of control, recognizing one's motivations, using principles of learning, and developing a curious mind.
http://www.und.nodak.edu/dept/ULC/rf-motiv.htm

The Emotion Home Page—index, basic, medium, links, graphics
Page introduces the topic of emotion and links to: introduction, a historical perspective on emotion, places and people, conferences, journals, on–line resources, and emotion research. http://emotion.salk.edu/emotion.html

Emotions and Emotional Intelligence—tutorial, basic, long, links, graphics
Covers the topic of emotional intelligence: what is emotional intelligence, emotions, methods for researching emotions, and references.
http://trochim.human.cornell.edu/gallery/young/emotion.htm

The Megahit Movies—index, interm., short, links, graphics
Large site that analyzes 20 movies (including *Raiders of the Lost Ark, Forrest Gump, Star Wars, E.T., Men in Black)* in detail. Analysis includes: characters, conflicts, plots, emotions, cinematic structures, and more.
http://www.mmsysgrp.com./megahits.htm

What's Your Emotional Intelligence Quotient?—interactive, basic, short, links, graphics
Page supporting Daniel Goleman's recent book, *Emotional Intelligence.* Users may take the quiz on–line here. http://www.utne.com/lens/bms/9bmseq.html

Research on Human Emotion—index, basic, medium, links
Page provides links to a variety of sources on emotion: physiology, temperament, emotion cognition, research projects, and a short summary of the three main theories of emotion.
http://www-white.media.mit.edu/vismod/demos/affect/AC_research/emotions.html

Theories

Human Behavior and Evolution Society—index, interm., short, links, graphics
Home page of a society devoted to exploring the evolutionary bases of human behavior including emotions and motivation. Page includes articles and tutorials on evolutionary psychology. http://psych.lmu.edu/hbes.htm

Interview: David Buss—article, interm., long, links, graphics
Interview with David Buss, author of *The Evolution of Desire* (1995) Buss is a contributor to the theory of evolutionary psychology.
http://www.lse.ac.uk/depts/cpnss/evolutionist/evobuss1.htm

Walter B. Cannon—text, basic, short, links
Short biography of Walter B. Cannon, whose work set the stage for the drive theory of motivation.
http://indy.radiology.uiowa.edu/Providers/Textbooks/SnyderMedHx/175Cannon.html

Homeostasis: General Principles—tutorial, interm., long, links, graphics
Discusses homeostasis and how it is achieved; also includes sections on feedback mechanisms and loops.
http://bioserve.latrobe.edu.au/vcebiol/cat1/aos2/u3aos21.html

Description of Maslow's Theory—tutorial, basic, search, links
Brief description of Maslow's theory and methodology.
http://snycorva.cortland.edu/~ANDERSMD/MASLOW/THEORY.HTML

Maslow's Hierarchy of Needs—graphic, basic, short, links, graphics
Graphic depicts the organization of Maslow's needs hierarchy.
http://www.coba.usf.edu/Marketing/Faculty/Kennedy/6-consum/sld011.htm

Maslow on Motivation—text, adv., long, links, graphics
Covers aspects of Maslow's thinking about motivation, includes sections on work, Blackfoot Indians, talent, human needs, gratification, quotes, and more.
http://www.ping.be/jvwit/Maslovmotivation.html

Motivation—tutorial, basic, short, links, graphics
Covers theories of motivation from a management perspective: Maslow's hierarchy of needs theory, theory x and theory y, three needs theory, goal setting theory, equity theory, and expectancy theory.
http://choo.fis.utoronto.ca/FIS/Courses/LIS1230/LIS1230sharma/motive1.htm

Theories of Emotion—tutorial, basic, long, links
Covers emotion theories briefly: James–Lange Theory, Cannon–Bard Theory, Lindsley's Arousal Theory, Schacter and Singer's Theory, and more.
http://www.people.memphis.edu/~clong/emotiont.htm

Hunger and Thirst

Arbor Nutrition Guide—index, basic, short, links, graphics, search
Comprehensive guide to food and nutrition, with links to food, clinical, food science, and other links. http://arborcom.com/

How Can You Control Your Hunger?—tutorial, basic, short, links, graphics
Tutorial on basics of eating and appetite, from a provider of dieting software.
http://www.dinesystems.com/control.htm

American Dietetic Association—index, basic, short, links, graphics, search
Home page of the American Dietetic Association (ADA) with links to nutrition resources, FAQ, hot topics, classified advertising, and others.
http://www.eatright.org/index.html

Moralization and Disgust—text, interm., short, links, graphics
Paul Rozin briefly lists the factors that lead to moralization and sanction of previously value–neutral items (i.e., cigarettes, meat, fat, and chocolate).
http://www.arise.org/roz3.html

Food and Pleasure—text, adv., long, links, graphics
Paul Rozin discusses cross–cultural relationships between food seen as pleasure or as nutrition. He concludes that American women derive the least pleasure from food while French men derive the most. http://www.arise.org/Rozin.html

Why, Yuck, That Does Sound Delicious—article, basic, long, links, graphics
Newspaper article about the wide variety of food items humans will eat.
http://www.freep.com/fun/food/qyucky17e.htm

More Americans Are Overweight—article, interm., long, links
From *Morbidity and Mortality* (1997), summarizes statistics for overweight Americans by age group. Concludes that obesity has risen significantly for all age groups since the last similar study in 1976–80.
http://www.newswise.com/articles/FATMMWR.CHS.html

Obesity: The World's Oldest Metabolic Disorder—tutorial, interm., long, links
Covers obesity from a medical point of view: indeces of overweight, assessment of body fat, obesity and arthritis, and more.
http://www.quantumhcp.com/obesity.htm

Food Finder—interactive, basic, short, links, graphics
Users may enter food items from fast food restaurants to learn nutritional information about them. http://www.olen.com/food/

Eating Disorders Website—index, basic, short, links, graphics
Home page of Eating Disorders Shared Awareness (EDSA), a self–help group for those afflicted with eating disorders. Links include anorexia nervosa, bulimia nervosa, compulsive overeating, signs and symptoms, physical dangers, and more. http://www.something-fishy.com/ed.htm

Diet and Weight Loss/Fitness—index, basic, long, links, graphics
Comprehensive page on diet and fitness includes sections on eating the right stuff, moving and exercising, FAQs, and links to other Web resources. http://www1.mhv.net/~donn/diet.html

Sexual Motives

Sex Ratios, United States, 1790–1990—animation, basic, short, links, graphics
Displays the number of males per 100 females in the United States over a 200 year period. http://www.ac.wwu.edu/~stephan/Animation/sexratios.html

The Kinsey Institute—index, basic, short, links, graphics
The home page of the Kinsey Institute links to library and collections, Kinsey clinics and training, events and exhibitions, and more. http://www.indiana.edu/~kinsey/

Cyberbods—graphic, basic, short, links, graphics
Illustrates five common sexual positions using abstract, robot–like, computer–graphic mannequins. http://www.sexscape.org/cyber/

Female Courtship Strategies—tutorial, adv., long, links
Discusses human female courtship strategies from an evolutionary perspective. http://world.topchoice.com/~psyche/love/strategy.html

Journal of Sex Research—journal, adv., long, links, graphics
Home page of the *Journal of Sex Research* provides call for papers, instructions for contributors, and tables of contents. http://www.ssc.wisc.edu/ssss/jsr.htm

Sexual Survey Results—text, basic, medium, links
Robert Wood Johnson Foundation (RWJF) sponsored sex survey results. (This is the survey commissioned in 1991 by the NIH but later halted by congressional political pressure, eventually completed with RWJF funding.) http://www.rwjf.org/library/win95ar2.htm

Basic Anatomy and Sexual Reproduction—tutorial, interm., short, links, graphics
From campus health service, has links to: the adult male, the adult female, and medical examinations. http://www.campuslife.utoronto.ca/services/sec/phy.html

About Pheromones—text, basic, short, links, graphics
Defines pheromones and provides examples from insects. http://www.nysaes.cornell.edu/pheronet/pherom.html

The Love Test—interactive, basic, short, links, graphics
Two tests users may take to assess their concept and/or experience of love.
http://topchoice.com/~psyche/lovetest/index.html

Marital Bliss—article, basic, medium, links, graphics
Reviews Buss and Shackleford's (1997) article on mate–retention strategies.
Authors maintain that men and women use different strategies to keep their
mates attracted to themselves.
http://www.allabouthealth.com/Current/News/Items2/news144.htm

Marital Bliss—text, interm., medium, links, graphics
Another summary of the Buss and Shackleford (1997) article, this one from APA.
http://www.apa.org/releases/bliss.html

Basic Information About Extramarital Affairs—tutorial, interm., long, links
From the book *The Monogamy Myth;* discusses why extramarital affairs occur.
http://www.vaughan-vaughan.com/affairs.html

Gays, Lesbians, and Bisexuals—FAQ, basic, short, links
Page answers questions about sexual orientation.
http://www.campuslife.utoronto.ca/services/sec/blg.html

On–line Sexual Disorders Screening Test for Men—interactive, basic, short,
links
Test diagnoses sexual motivation in men, scores automatically.
http://www.med.nyu.edu/Psych/screens/sdsm.html

On–line Sexual Disorders Screening Test for Women—interactive, basic, short,
links
Test diagnoses sexual motivation in women; scores automatically.
http://www.med.nyu.edu/Psych/screens/sdsf.html

Sexual Orientation and Homosexuality—FAQ, basic, medium, links, graphics
From APA, answers basic questions about sexual orientation and homosexuality.
http://www.apa.org/pubinfo/orient.html

Achievement

Motivational Factors in Routine Performance—interactive, interm., short, links,
graphics
Simulation from EXPERSIM allows users to manipulate variables of interest in
motivation and then make conclusions based on the matrix of variables selected.
http://samiam.colorado.edu/~mcclella/expersim/intromotivational.html

Emotional Experience

What is Emotion?—tutorial, basic, long, links, graphics
Covers aspects of emotion and has linked examples throughout. Has six photos of
models displaying emotions and covers major models of emotion.
http://psych.wisc.edu/faculty/pages/croberts/topic8.html

The Emotional Brain—article, basic, short, links, graphics
From NIH Record, discusses the lessons of fear conditioning in revealing how
emotions work. http://www.nih.gov/news/NIH-Record/06_03_97/story04.htm

Our Emotions—article, basic, short, links, graphics
From the *Los Angeles Times,* article about how emotions work. Sidebar contains a
basic glossary.
http://www.latimes.com/HOME/NEWS/SCIENCE/REPORTS/THEBRAIN/
emote.htm

The Amygdala Home Page—index, interm., short, links, graphics, Java
Page by researcher contains information about and links to other pages on the
amygdala. http://marlin.utmb.edu/~nkeele/

The Validity of Polygraph Examinations—text, basic, short, links, graphics
Page provides summary and table about the validity of polygraph examinations
and concludes most are not valid. http://www.apa.org/releases/liedetector.html

Polygraph Law Resource Page—index, adv., long, links
Page attempts to keep up with recent federal and state court rulings on the use of
polygraph evidence in courtrooms. http://truth.idbsu.edu/polygraph/polylaw.html

Lie Detector Tests—text, basic, short, links, graphics
From the Department of Labor, information about the Polygraph Protection Act of
1988, which prohibited the use of the polygraph in most business settings.
http://www.dol.gov/dol/asp/public/programs/handbook/eppa.htm

Lie Detector Tests—tutorial, basic, short, links, graphics
From a guide for starting a small business, this page discusses basic laws about
polygraphs and features a clickable map of the United States so that users may
find any applicable state laws on polygraph examinations.
http://www.toolkit.cch.com/text/P05_1035.htm

Controlling Anger—text, basic, long, links, graphics
From APA, discusses anger and some strategies for its control.
http://www.apa.org/pubinfo/anger.html

James, Aristotle, and Sartre on Emotion—text, interm., short, links, graphics
Page provides capsule views on how each looked at emotion.
http://www.cns.nyu.edu/home/ledoux/authors.html

Just for Fun

Pleasure Quiz—interactive, basic, medium, links, graphics
Users may take and score quiz on life satisfaction. Page contains links to
information about results and research about the quiz.
http://www.arise.org/quiz.html

Food Quiz—interactive, basic, medium, links, graphics
From the Mayo Clinic, asks five questions about the calories and fat of common
holiday food items. Answers are provided.
http://www.mayohealth.org/mayo/9411/htm/quiz_sb.htm

Motivation Self Quiz—interactive, basic, short, links
Users may take a ten–item self quiz on motivation; provides instant feedback.
http://beowulf.simplynet.net/ejones/PsyTest/ch09mcq.htm

JC's ChileWeb—index, basic, medium, links, graphics
Page has information on chile peppers, capsaicin, and links to other sites on chiles.
http://www.wenet.net/~carrasco/chileweb.htm

You Put What in Your Mouth?—interactive, basic, long, links, graphics
Inspired by Schwabe's book *Unmentionable Cuisine* (1979), staffers at this Web
site volunteer their most disgusting ingestions and invite users to do the same.
http://www.monster.com/pf/mb/client/ui/communit/roar/reviews/02-97/gross.htm

Emotion Detector—interactive, basic, medium, links
Asks 26 questions about how users would handle behavior of their significant
other and then scores it. (Not scientifically valid.)
http://denver.digitalcity.com/cgi-bin/determinator

The Entrepeneur Test—interactive, basic, short, links, graphics
Ten–item test that measures need for achievement in business setting. Users may
see how achievement motivated they are. http://www.liraz.com/webquiz.htm

Community Sparkplugs—interactive, basic, long, links
Discussion and quiz about "community sparkplugs" or people who are more likely
to become involved in community activities, and the likelihood of such involvement.
http://www.crisny.org/not-for-profit/thetute/STEP/SPARKREP.HTM

Egg Faces—graphic, basic, short, graphics
A photo of twelve human emotional facial expressions drawn on eggs.
http://www.teleport.com/~bcat/gallery_g1_5.html

The Smiley Dictionary—index, basic, short, links, graphics
Provides information about smileys (or emoticons), the simple graphics used in
e–mail to denote the emotional state of the sender.
http://www.netsurf.org/~violet/Smileys/

12

Human Development

Human development is a vast area of psychology covering topics from the newest areas in biology to the deepest philosophical issues of life and death. Below are listed URLs of interest to students of human development. The URLs are grouped by the categories of: General Resources in Development; Theories of Development; Prenatal Development; Childhood; Adolescence; Adulthood; and Just for Fun.

General Resources in Development

Disney's Family.Com Page—index, basic, short, links, graphics, search
This commercial site is designed for families and contains links to the following categories: activities, computing, food, health, learning, local affiliates, parenting, and travel. The site contains many colorful graphics and animations. In addition, content changes daily with features on parenting, recipes, and seasonal activities. http://www.family.com/

Virtual Stand for Children—index, basic, short, links, graphics
This is the home page of Stand for Children, a national child advocacy group, with links to their newsletter, local chapters, and to seasonally–changing items (i.e., holiday cards, meetings). http://www.stand.org/

On–line Mendelian Inheritance in Man (OMIM)—index, interm., short, links, search
From the National Institutes of Health (NIH), this page provides access to detailed information on human genetics. Users may access the OMIM database and look up nearly any piece of information in human genetics. Links are also provided to other related databases—one of the benefits of the human genome project. http://www3.ncbi.nlm.nih.gov/Omim/

National Parent Information Network—index, interm., short, links, search
Sponsored by two ERIC clearinghouses, Elementary and Early Childhood Education and Urban Education, this page's purpose is " ...to provide information to parents and those who work with parents and to foster the exchange of parenting materials." The site includes Parent News, Urban/Minority Families, Parents AskERIC, the PARENTING discussion list, and other materials. http://ericps.ed.uiuc.edu/npin/npinhome.html

Parenthood Web—index, basic, medium, links, graphics, search
A comprehensive site for parents that includes features: In the Spotlite, What's New, Facts and Figures, Chat, and Product Recalls. http://www.parenthoodweb.com/

entsPlace.com—index, basic, medium, links, graphics, search
A site that started with the birth of a baby, Noah. Noah's parents realized they needed help and it was hard to find. Thus, they started ParentsPlace. The site has many links to chats, forums, and other resources for parents and children. http://www.parentsplace.com/

Human Relations Publications—index, basic, medium, links, search
Large index site on human relations from the University of Missouri Outreach and Extension Service. More than 50 topics cover the entire span of human development including toilet training, motor development, HIV/AIDS, choosing day care, and death and dying.
http://muextension.missouri.edu/xplor/hesguide/humanrel/

Parent Soup—index, basic, medium, links, graphics, search
Another commercial site devoted to parents includes sections for parents of all ages of children. Site also has chats, surveys, and other interactive features. http://www.parentsoup.com/

The Parent's Page—index, basic, medium, links
Comprehensive site full of links for expectant couples and new parents. http://www.efn.org/~djz/birth/babylist.html

The Child Abuse Yellow Pages—index, basic, short, links, graphics, search
A site where users can report child abuse, see pictures of missing children, chat with other parents, and do other related things. http://idealist.com/cayp/

Child Development—index, basic, long, links, graphics
Comprehensive index page with articles (viewable and downloadable) on development: infant, toddler, preschooler, school–age, intellectual, emotional/social, ages and stages series, brain development, and others. http://www.exnet.iastate.edu/Pages/nncc/Child.Dev/child.dev.page.html

KidSource On–line—index, basic, medium, links, graphics, search
Comprehensive index page with health care and education information for parents and children: services, new articles, product recalls, collections, and featured article. http://www.kidsource.com/

Theories of Development

Classic Theories of Child Development—index, basic, medium, links
Developmental theories of Margaret Mahler, Sigmund Freud, and Erik Erikson. Page has links to information on the three theorists, to age–based patterns of development, and to related sites. Site is part of Child Development page. http://idealist.com/children/cdw.html

Constructivist Theories—tutorial, interm., short, links
Differentiates between social (i.e.,Vygotsky) and cognitive (i.e., Piaget) versions of constructivist theories. http://www.coe.uh.edu/~srmehall/theory/construct.html

The Minnesota Twin Family Study—text, interm., medium, links, search
Describes some of the famous twin studies conducted at the University of
Minnesota–Twin Cities by David Lykken and his colleagues: Minnesota Twin
Registry, Minnesota Twin Study of Adult Development, and Minnesota Twin
Family Study (both Male and Female Projects).
http://cla.umn.edu/psych/psylabs/mtfs/tfsindex.htm

Jean Piaget Archives: Biography—text, interm., medium, graphics
Biography of Jean Piaget with five photos from birth to old age.
http://www.unige.ch/piaget/biog.html

Vygotsky Centennial Project—index, interm., medium, links, graphics
A page celebrating the centennial of Vygotsky's birth by requesting submissions on
the topic of mediation. Two such submissions are on the page presently: the role of
culture in Vygotskyean–informed psychology; and talk of saying, showing,
gesturing, and feeling in Wittgenstein and Vygotsky. The site also has links to
other Vygotsky–related pages.
http://www.massey.ac.nz/~ALock/virtual/project2.html

Kohlberg's Moral Stages—text, basic, short
Outline of Kohlberg's stages of moral development with short descriptions of each.
http://www.awa.com/w2/erotic_computing/kohlberg.stages.html

Attachment Theory—tutorial, interm., medium, links, graphics
Discusses attachment styles, imprinting, attachment, and Ainsworth and
Bowlby's work on attachment styles including the strange situation.
http://galton.psych.nwu.edu/GreatIdeas/attachment.html

Constructivism and Adult Education—tutorial, basic, short, links
Page contains links to theoretical overviews and historic background, what is the
nature of learning, the learning environment, and other related items.
http://www.public.iastate.edu/~rmartin/Constructivism1/0-contents.htm

Prenatal Development

The First Nine Months—table, basic, short, links, graphics
Lists the highlights of prenatal development.
http://www.ptiweb.com/~cpc/9months.htm

The Fetal Senses—article, interm., long, links
Discusses sensory development *in utero*: sensitivity to touch, the fetus in motion,
tasting and smelling, listening and hearing, development of vision, senses in
action, and references.
http://www.birthpsychology.com/lifebefore/fetalsense.html

Birth Psychology—index, basic, short, links, graphics
Home page of the Association for Pre– and Perinatal Psychology and Health
(APPPAH), has links to life before birth, origins of violence, the birth scene, healing
of pre– and perinatal trauma, and others.
http://www.birthpsychology.com/index.html

Image Gallery/Obstetrics—graphic, interm., long, links, graphics
Provides six ultrasound images (some are color enhanced) of the fetus *in utero*. Images include third–trimester profile, umbilical cord artery, 24–week fetus, and others. http://www.acuson.com/5.imagegallery/5_3/5_3.html#5_3_5

The Bradley Method—index, basic, medium, links, graphics
The home page of the Bradley Method, a form of spouse–assisted childbirth, provides links to goals, diet, training, and other aspects of the method. http://www.bradleybirth.com/

Baby Bag Online—index, basic, short, links, graphics
Comprehensive index page with links to all aspects of pregnancy and childbirth; includes product recalls, regular departments, and an interactive section. http://www.babybag.com/index.htm

Pregnancy Testing Kits—index, basic, short, links, graphics
Part of an on–line drug store, this section offers information on ten commonly available pregnancy tests; users may see how to interpret the results. http://software2.bu.edu/COHIS/ylds/pregtest/pregtest.htm

Breastfeeding Answers—index, basic, medium, links, graphics
Answers nine commonly asked questions about breastfeeding, including human milk's properties, breastfeeding in public, breastfeeding and work, and others. http://www.ecrknox.com/betz/question.htm

California Cryobank—index, interm., short, links
The home page of a reproductive tissue facility. The site advertises its services, including frozen semen and embryo storage, stem cell storage, and other reproductive services. Users may search the site for semen–donor profiles. The site has links to other sites and information on similar reproductive technologies. http://www.cryobank.com/

Assisted Reproductive Technologies—text, interm., medium
Provides information on in vitro fertilization (IVF), gamete intrafallopian transfer (GIFT), zygote intrafallopian transfer (ZIFT), and frozen embryos. The page is linked to a reproductive services clinic in San Francisco. http://www.ihr.com/bafertil/assistre.html

Childhood

I Am Your Child—index, basic, short, links, graphics
Information for parents of young children (0–3 years of age): key issues, brain facts, parent questions, ages and stages, expert advice, and more. http://www.iamyourchild.org/start.html

Childhood Immunization Schedule 1997—text, adv., medium, links
From the AAFP (American Academy of Family Physicians). Text and tables show the recommended schedule for regular and catch up vaccinations. Specific recommendations for HBsAg–negative/positive/unknown mothers are listed as is a July 1997 update about polio vaccines. http://www.aafp.org/family/pracguid/rep-520.html

Home "Safe" Home—tutorial, basic, medium, links, graphics
Tutorial from the University of Texas Medical Branch on how to make your home safe. The tutorial uses a house's rooms as a model for its lessons: Baby's Room, Bathroom, Bedroom, Child's Room, Living Room, Dining Room, Kitchen, Garage, and Backyard.
http://www.utmb.edu/mmlab/safetya.html

Sesame Street Parents—text, adv., long
Physical development from birth to 11 is described by experts from Harvard Medical School, the University of Maryland, and Columbia University College of Physicians and Surgeons. http://ctw.org/parents/weekly/0496/049604t1.htm

Choosing Quality Child Care—index, basic, medium, links
Provides information from the National Network for Child Care on issues related to quality child care: your home, day care home, child care center, school, and preparing your child.
http://www.exnet.iastate.edu/Pages/nncc/Choose.Quality.Care/qual.care.page.htm

Lies Parents Tell About Why They Work—article, basic, long, links, graphics, search
U.S. News article (May 12, 1997) about parents who stay at home to parent and those who do not. Lies are: Lie #1: We need the extra money. Lie #2: Day care is perfectly good. Lie #3: Inflexible companies are the key problem Lie #4: Dads would gladly stay home. Lie #5: High taxes force both of us to work.
http://www.usnews.com/usnews/issue/970512/12wor.htm

Cultural Diversity and Early Education—index, adv., long, links
Report of a workshop by the National Academy of Science. Topics covered: cultural contexts for learning, cultural diversity at home, what children bring to school, implications for early education, and directions for research.
http://www.nap.edu/readingroom/books/earlyed/contents.html

Fonetix—tutorial, adv., long, links, graphics, search, Java
Highly interactive site covers articulations, reading skills, sign language, pronunciation, and diagnostics. The page also has quizzes, CU–SeeMe, a glossary, and experiments. http://www.ee.umanitoba.ca/~morawej/Speech/

Project No Spank—index, basic, long, links, graphics
A page devoted to the cessation of spanking as a method of discipline. Includes links to articles, letters, news, and e–mail replies to its policy of no spanking.
http://silcon.com/~ptave/toc.htm

Guidelines for Spanking Your Children—text, basic, medium, links
An Evangelical Christian page promoting the proper use of spanking.
http://www.gelservices.com/spank.html

National Pediculosis Association—index, basic, short, links, graphics
Home page of the National Pediculosis Association; provides links to news, FAQs, good stuff, participate, and contacts; also sells the LiceMeister nit comb.
http://www.headlice.org

.nddle Childhood Network—index, adv., medium, links
Research on middle childhood sponsored by the MacArthur Foundation. Current research initiatives are: Joint Task Force on Family Processes, Ethnicity and Ethnic Identity in Middle Childhood, MacArthur Transitions Study: CCDP Follow–Up, New Hope Family and Child Component, California Childhoods: Institutions, Contexts and Pathways of Development, Exploration of Empirical Pathways in Middle Childhood, History of Authority, and others.
http://midchild.soe.umich.edu/

temperament.com—index, interm., short, links
Sponsored by the publishers of the Carey Temperament Scales, devoted to behavioral individuality; links to FAQs, readings, clinical use of the test, and other related items. http://www.temperament.com/

Adolescence

Mental Health Risk Factors for Adolescents—index, basic, long, links
Page has links to 19 resources relevant to adolescent development: abuse, alcohol and other drugs, eating disorders, suicide, and more.
http://education.indiana.edu/cas/adol/mental.html

Do's and Don'ts for Divorcing Parents—text, basic, short, links
From Family Law Adviser, a page from a law firm's advice section on divorce. Provides useful advice for parents who are divorcing.
http://www.divorcenet.com/ny/nyart09.html

Topics on Sexuality and Relationships—index, basic, medium, links
From the University of Toronto's Sexual Education and Peer Counselling Centre, this page has links to many topics in the area of dating, sex, and relationships. Topics include: birth control, STDs, lesbian, gay and bisexual issues, basic human anatomy and physiology, and relationship issues.
http://www.campuslife.utoronto.ca/services/sec/bc.html

All About Condoms—index, basic, medium, links, animation
Page from the Rubber Tree, a seller of condoms: how to choose a condom, how to use a condom (choice of static or animated link), and effectiveness of condoms.
http://cn.org/rt/howtouse.htm

Parental Satisfaction with Eighth Grade—article, adv., medium
Report from the Department of Education on parental satisfaction on education of their eighth graders. http://www.ed.gov/pubs/OR/ResearchRpts/parents.html

How *Seventeen* Undermines Young Women—article, basic, medium, links, graphics
On–line article from *EXTRA!* castigating the magazine *Seventeen* for promoting superficial values in adolescent females.
http://www.econet.apc.org/fair/extra/best-of-extra/seventeen.html

Career Mosaic—index, basic, short, links, graphics
A site where employers and applicants can meet on the Web with sections for posting resumes, specific companies, job listings, and links to other sites.
http://www.careermosaic.com/

What Works for Girls—text, basic, short, links, graphics
From the American Association of University Women (AAUW), a short summary of recent research about what kinds of environmental variables contribute positively to the development of healthy and well–adjusted girls.
http://www.aauw.org/4000/lessonslearned.html

Adolescent Depression–FAQ, basic, medium, links, graphics
Answers basic questions about depression in adolescents.
http://www.mentalhealth.com/mag1/p51-dp01.html

Eating Disorders—tutorial, basic, short, links, graphics
Page provides information and advice about dealing with eating disorders: what is an eating disorder, who gets an eating disorder, what causes an eating disorder, common risk factors, and related conditions.
http://www.laureate.com/abouted.html

Adulthood

Internet Herald—publication, basic, medium, links, graphics, search
A Web publication (monthly) devoted to Generation X issues. Site has regular columns and feature sections. http://www.iherald.com/

ADA Accessibility Guidelines—index, adv., long, links, graphics
The complete ADA guidelines. The site has 10 linked sections for easy searching.
http://www.access-board.gov/bfdg/adaag.htm

Our Best Years—publication, basic, medium, links, graphics
Home page for *Midlife Moments,* the Web version of newspaper columns by Mike Bellah. He writes from Canyon, Texas. http://www.bestyears.com/index.html

MIDMAC—index, interm., medium, links
The MacArthur Foundation Research Network on Successful Midlife Development's home page of a major study on middle age. Page has links to research, books and publications, bulletins, article about project, and an index.
http://midmac.med.harvard.edu/midmac.html

Social Security Online—index, interm., medium, links, graphics, search
The official home page of the Social Security Administration. The site contains news, FAQs, services, forms, and many other features. http://www.ssa.gov/

The AARP Webplace—index, basic, medium, links, graphics, search
Home page of the AARP, the American Association of Retired Persons: news, links for information, community programs, advocacy, and membership and benefits.
http://www.aarp.org/

Planning Tools—interactive, basic, medium, links, graphics
An index page to a set of interactive financial tools and downloadable spreadsheets. Tools include Mortgage Refinancing Worksheet, Home Equity Loan Worksheet, Personal Loan Calculator, Sensible Credit Calculator, Auto Loan Calculator, Education Services Worksheet, Retirement Planning Worksheet, Personal Balance Worksheet, and Letter of Credit Flowchart.
http://www.corestates.com/04-pt.html

Compassionate Friends National Page—index, basic, short, links, graphics
The home page of a group devoted to the grief of parents. Site has links to chat with other parents, e–mail, FAQs, local chapter locator, brochures, and other sites. http://longhorn.jjt.com/~tcf_national/

Webster's Death, Dying, and Grief Guide—index, basic, medium, links, graphics
A large index page of Web resources on death, dying, and grief with links to grief and healing resources, depression, hospices, survivors, and many other death–related topics. http://www.katsden.com/death/index.html

Atlas of United States Mortality—index, interm., medium, links, graphics, search
From the Centers for Disease Control, this site offers .pdf format (Adobe Acrobat) color maps. Available maps include deaths due to heart disease, cancers, motor vehicle accidents, and others. http://www.cdc.gov/nchswww/products/pubs/pubd/other/atlas/atlas.htm

Just for Fun

Babies—interactive, basic, medium, links, graphics
Users may try this short quiz about basic facts about babies. http://www.questionmark.com/qmwebquestions/babies.htm

Personality

Some psychologists believe that personality is the most exciting area of psychology, and a few even start their general psychology courses with this chapter. Whatever one's psychological subfield is, it is hard to argue that personality is not interesting. This chapter covers personality from the classic psychodynamic theories inspired by Freud and his successors, through the humanistic revolution inspired by Rogers and Maslow, to the modern biological and trait formulations of personality. Personality tests and cross–cultural differences in personality are also covered. The URLs are grouped by the categories of: General Resources in Personality; Psychodynamic Theories; Humanistic Theories; Biological Theories; Modern Theories; Personality Tests; Cross–Cultural Aspects; and Just for Fun.

General Resources in Personality

The Personality Project—index, basic, short, links
Page guides users to current literature in personality. Links include: personality research literature, recommended readings, personal Web sites, psychological organizations, personality graduate programs, and more.
http://pmc.psych.nwu.edu:80/personality.html

Great Ideas in Personality—index, basic, short, links
Site covers scientific research programs in personality: psychoanalysis, behaviorism, sociobiology, attachment theory, interpersonal theory, five–factor model, psychoticism–extraversion–neuroticism, basic emotions, cognitive social learning, and intelligence. http://galton.psych.nwu.edu/GreatIdeas.html

Personality and Consciousness—index, basic, short, links, graphics
Page covers personality theorists and other personality–related issues. Theorists are: Adler, Bruhn, Freud, Jung, Kelly, Lewin, Maslow, Rogers, Skinner, and Tart.
http://www.wynja.com/personality/theorists.html

The American Psychoanalytic Foundation—index, interm., medium, links, graphics
The home page of the American Psychoanalytic Foundation, with links to psychoanalytic institutes and societies, programs and future projects, parent–child centers, and more. http://www.cyberpsych.org/apf.htm

Personality Processes—article, adv., long, links
Annual Review of Psychology article on personality includes sections on recent trends, species typical behavior, individual differences and similarities, unique patterns of behavior, and more.
http://pmc.psych.nwu.edu/revelle/publications/AR.html

Psychodynamic Theories

The Personality Project—index, interm., short, links, search
Page for users interested in personality theory, with links to readings, psychometrics, professional societies, graduate programs in personality, and others. Page also has several search engine links preset to personality. http://fas.psych.nwu.edu/personality.html or http://pmc.psych.nwu.edu/personality

The Freud Web—index, basic, short, links, graphics
Page contains categories of cultural context, theory of the mind, and techniques. It also has links to a biography and chronology of Freud's life. http://www.stg.brown.edu/projects/hypertext/landow/HTatBrown/freud/Freud_OV.html

FreudNet: The A.A. Brill Library—index, basic, short, links, graphics
Web site of the Brill Library of Psychoanalysis; contains links to material on Freud, psychoanalysis, the American Psychoanalytic Association, and others. http://plaza.interport.net/nypsan/

Sigmund Freud Museum Vienna—index, interm., short, links, graphics
Home page of his museum in Vienna, contains links to chronology, themes, topography, media library, and more. http://freud.t0.or.at/freud/e/navigate.htm

The Freud Museum of London—index, interm., short, links, graphics
Home page of the Freud Museum of London, has links to introduction, hours and fees, and other related sites. http://www.dalton.org/students/DBS/freud/index.html

Freud's Stages of Development—tutorial, basic, short, links
Provides capsule descriptions of Freud's stages of development: oral, anal, phallic, latency, and genital. http://idealist.com/children/freud.html

Psychoanalysis—tutorial, interm., short, links, graphics
Clickable image map and other links lead to information about the structure of psychoanalysis and other aspects of Freud's thought. Topics include the success of therapy, constructions, universal generalizations, and more. http://galton.psych.nwu.edu/GreatIdeas/psychoanalysis.html

Psychoanalysis—article, adv., long
Full text of the 1926 *Encyclopedia Britannica* (13th ed.) entry under "psychoanalysis." Written by Sigmund Freud. http://www.haverford.edu/psych109/freud.psa.html

Psychoanalysis and Psychodynamic Topics—index, basic, long, links, graphics
From Mental Health Net, a list of rated links in psychoanalysis and related topics; includes Web resources, news groups, mailing lists, journals, professional organizations, and more. http://www.cmhc.com/guide/pro11.htm

C.G. Jung, Analytical Psychology, and Culture—index, basic, medium, links, graphics, search
This page has links to a wide variety of links about Jung. They include announcements of meetings, a glossary of terms, and others. http://www.cgjung.com/

The Jung Index—index, basic, medium, links, graphics, search
> The page claims, " The Jung Index's mission is to connect you to the world of Jungian/Analytical Psychology. It is a gathering place for professionals in fields of academia as far ranging as Clinical Psychology, Mythology, and Neurobiology." http://www.jungindex.net/

Carl Jung: Anthology—index, interm., short, links, graphics
> Page provides links to fragments of original writings by Jung on a variety of topics, including archetypes, collective unconcious, ego, shadow, and more. http://www.enteract.com/~jwalz/Jung/

JungWeb—index, interm., long, links
> Comprehensive page for Jungian psychology features calendar of events, dreams, JUNG–PSYC (a mailing list), articles, and more. http://www.onlinepsych.com/jungweb/

Classical Adlerian Psychology—index, basic, long, links, graphics
> From the Adler Institute of San Francisco, page has links to readings, demonstrations, graphics, biographies, and more. http://ourworld.compuserve.com:80/homepages/hstein/

Karen Horney—index, basic, medium, links, graphics
> Page has brief linked biography of Horney and links to related sites. http://www.1w.net/karen/

Psychiatry Information for the General Public—index, basic, long, links, graphics
> From a school of medicine, contains links to on–line screening tests, diagnosis, treatment, and to other related links. http://www.med.nyu.edu/Psych/public.html

Defense Mechanisms and Unconscious Causes of Fear—tutorial, basic, long, links, graphics
> Lists and explains ten defense mechanisms and then discusses the origin of unconscious fears. http://www.cmhc.com/psyhelp/chap5/chap5j.htm

Humanistic Theories

Humanistic Psychology—text, basic, long, links, graphics, search
> From the Association of Humanist Psychology (AHP), page discusses the recent history and future prospects of humanistic psychology. http://ahpweb.org/aboutahp/whatis.html

Allen Turner's Person–Centered Web Site—index, interm., short, links, graphics
> Page on person–centered psychology includes links to other person–centered links, publications, associations, information for students, and more. http://users.powernet.co.uk/pctmk/

Association for Humanistic Psychology (AHP)—index, basic, medium, links, graphics
> Home page of the AHP links to About Humanistic Psychology, AHP in Action, People, related links, and more. http://pmc.psych.nwu.edu:80/personality.html

Carl Rogers—tutorial, basic, short, links, graphics
Page contains a short biography of Carl Rogers and discusses his approach to psychology. http://www1.rider.edu/~suler/rogers.html

Carl Rogers—tutorial, basic, short, links, graphics
Another short biography of Rogers with additional information about his methods of therapy. http://psy1.clarion.edu/jms/Rogers.html

Carl Rogers's Ten Principles of Learning—text, basic, short, links
Page lists Rogers's ten principles for learning.
http://www.wisc.edu/depd/html/un2tab1.htm

Abraham Maslow—tutorial, short, basic, links
Discusses Maslow's hierarchy of needs and his influence on modern psychology.
http://www.utoledo.edu/homepages/ddavis/maslow.htm

Maslow Publications—index, adv., medium, links, graphics
Contains lists of publications by or about Maslow: books in print by Maslow, books in print about Maslow, out–of–print books, audio/visual materials, articles by Maslow, and more. http://www.maslow.com/index.html

Aphorisms Galore: Maslow—text, basic, short, links, graphics, search
Page has a saying by Maslow: "When the only tool you have is a hammer...."
http://www.aphorismsgalore.com/author/Abraham_Maslow.html

Biological Theories

The Four Humors—tutorial, basic, short, links, graphics
Explains the words: phlegmatic, sanguine, melancholic, and choleric. Shows how they derived from Hippocrates's theory of personality.
http://www.parlez.com/word-of-the-day/humors.html

The Three Body Types—tutorial, basic, short, links
Describes the characteristics of Sheldon's somatotypes.
http://www.fitnesszone.com/features/archives/body-types.html

Hans Eysenck—text, basic, short, links, graphics
Short biography of the late biological–personality theorist, Hans Eysenck.
http://www.psych101.com/bio/eysenck.html

Hans Eysenck—text, interm., medium, links
Another short biography of the late Hans Eysenck; discusses his work.
http://152.52.2.152/newsroom/ntn/health/090897/health8_29468_noframes.html

Biological Dimensions of Personality—tutorial, interm., medium, links
Presents biological–personality approach based on the PEN (psychoticism, extraversion, neuroticism) model. Page consists of a table with the PEN headings as columns and theorists as rows. Links in the table provide information about a theorist's interpretation of a trait.
http://galton.psych.nwu.edu/GreatIdeas/pen.html

The Minnesota Twin Family Study—text, interm., medium, links, search
Describes some of the famous twin studies conducted at the University of
Minnesota—Twin Cities by David Lykken, and his colleagues. Site includes:
Minnesota Twin Registry, Minnesota Twin Study of Adult Development,
Minnesota Twin Family Study (both Male and Female Projects).
http://cla.umn.edu/psych/psylabs/mtfs/tfsindex.htm

Modern Theories

Locus of Control—text, basic, short, links, graphics
Page provides short definition of locus of control and discusses agency and the self.
http://www.ncrel.org/skrs/areas/issues/students/learning/lr2locus.htm

Locus of Control and Attributional Style Inventory—interactive, basic, long,
links, graphics
Users may take this test to get results on their success attributional style and
failure attributional style. Test is scored automatically.
http://www.queendom.com/lc.html

Measuring Sensation Seeking—text, basic, short
Brief description of Zuckerman's concept of sensation seeking and its behaviors.
http://165.112.78.61/NIDA_Notes/NNVol10N4/MeasureSens.html

Novel Ads and Sensation Seekers—article, interm., medium, links, graphics
From *NIDA Notes,* discusses research on ad campaign showing that teen drug
abuse might be lowered by substituting other types of thrill–seeking activities.
http://www.nida.nih.gov/NIDA_Notes/NNVol10N4/Sensation.html

"Extreeeme"—article, basic, long, links, graphics
From *U.S. News,* article discusses the new trends in extreme sports: skydiving,
rollerblading, skateboarding, and others. Article covers motivations of participants,
risks, and research. http://www.usnews.com/usnews/issue/970630/30extr.htm

Personal Construct Psychology—index, interm., long, links, graphics
Page covers George Kelly's personal construct psychology and has links to a list
server, related Web links, *Journal of Constructivist Psychology*, meeting
announcements, and more. http://ksi.cpsc.ucalgary.ca/PCP/PCP.html

Interpersonal Theory—tutorial, interm., short, links, graphics
Discusses the aspects of complementarity and circumplex structure in the
interpersonal theory derived from the ideas of Harry Stack Sullivan, George Herbert
Mead, and Timothy Leary. Has links to other Web sources on interpersonal theory.
http://galton.psych.nwu.edu/GreatIdeas/interpersonal.html

The Interpersonal Circumplex—index, interm., medium, links, graphics
Contains resources for theory and research in the interpersonal circumplex theory
of personality. http://www.uwp.edu/academic/psychology/faculty/netcirc.htm

The Big Five Factors of Personality—tutorial, basic, short, links, graphics
Gives short descriptions of the big five personality traits: neuroticism, extroversion,
openness to experience, agreeableness, and conscientiousness.
http://www.psych-test.com/bigfive.htm

The Big Five Dimensions—tutorial, interm., long, links
> Provides a table with the big five personality traits (extroversion, agreeableness, conscientiousness, stability, openness) as columns and theorists as rows. Links in the table provide information about a theorist's interpretation of a trait. http://galton.psych.nwu.edu/GreatIdeas/bigfive.html

The Big Five Taxonomy—tutorial, adv., long, links
> Answers: 1) What is the evidence on which the claim that there are five basic traits rests?; 2) Summarize the major conceptual and empirical work relevant to the nature and usefulness of these dimensions?; and 3) Discuss whether this system fully captures what is meant by "personality." http://fujita.iusb.edu/big5.html

International Personality Item Pool (IPIP)—index, adv., long, links
> Page represents an attempt to develop a "collaboratory," a computer–based system that allows scientists to work together without geographical barriers. The page's main focus is the development of the IPIP, a test designed to measure personality using the big five model. http://ipip.ori.org/ipip/index.htm

The Emerging Synthesis in Personality Psychology—article, adv., long, links, graphics
> *Contemporary Psychology* review of Lykken's *The Antisocial Personalities* (1995); discusses the current state of personality theories. States, " It is hard to imagine that this book...could have been published in the 1970s." http://www.apa.org/journals/cnt/dec96/lykken.html

Personality Tests

Personality Tests on the WWW—index, basic, short, links, graphics
> Offers 21 links to on–line personality tests. Includes tests for type–A personality, left or right brain, assertiveness, and others. http://www.2h.com/Tests/personality.phtml

Spending Personality Self–Test—interactive, basic, medium, links
> Page contains on–line version of commercially available test users may take in order to analyze their spending habits. http://www.ns.net/cash/selftest/selftest.html

Somatic Inkblot Series—index, adv., short, links, graphics
> Home page of the Somatic Inkblot Series, dedicated to the use of projective techniques. The page has links to sample inkblots, a journal, membership information, and others. http://www.owt.com/sis/

Keirsey Temperament Sorter—interactive, interm., long, links
> Users may take this personality test based upon Jung's theories. The test yields 16 combinations of personality types. http://www.keirsey.com/cgi-bin/keirsey/newkts.cgi

Axiom Software Ltd.—index, basic, short, links, graphics
> Home page of provider of personality–profiling test, DISC, page has links to information on personality profiling and other topics. http://www.axiomsoftware.com/default.htm

The Personality Tests—index, basic, short, links, graphics, Java
Links to on–line interactive personality tests includes: Keirsey Temperament Sorter, Enneagram, Personality Profile, Color Test, and the Maykorner Test (requires Java). http://www.freshy.com/personality/index2.html

Cross–Cultural Aspects

Japanese View of Self: Is it Unique?—article, basic, long, links, graphics
From the *Japan Labor Bulletin,* article (1994) explores the differences in Western and Japanese views of the self (i.e., independent vs. interdependent). http://www.mol.go.jp/jil/bulletin/year/1994/vol33-03/04.htm

Psychological Science in a Cultural Context—article, adv., long, links, graphics
From lead author's pages, draft version of *American Psychologist* article on cross–cultural effects. Includes sections: Towards Indigenous Indian Psychology, Psychology in the Maori Context, Bridge of Troubled Waters: a Turkish Vision, and in Speaking Together. http://www.swarthmore.edu/SocSci/kgergen1/text2.html

Just for Fun

Psychtoons—graphic, basic, medium, links, graphics
From *Self Help and Psychology Magazine,* page displays cartoon and has selections to other cartoons on mental health and personality topics. http://cybertowers.com/selfhelp/psychtoons/index.html

Barbarian's On–line Test Page—interactive, basic, medium, links, graphics
A collection of serious and not–so–serious tests, including intelligence tests, personality tests, fun tests, and others. http://www.iglobal.net/psman/prstests.html

That's My Theory: Freud—interactive, basic, short, links, graphics
From the PBS series *A Science Odyssey*, page allows users to explore psychoanalytic theory via the metaphor of a TV game show as they ask three different "Freud's" questions about his theory. http://www.pbs.org/wgbh/aso/mytheory/freud/

Abnormal Behavior

The problems of abnormal behavior are of great interest to students and professionals. Indeed, the area of abnormal psychology is one of the field's largest. Classification of abnormal patterns of behavior is covered in this chapter, as are legal issues and suicide. The URLs are grouped by the categories of: General Resources in Abnormal Psychology; Models, Criteria, and Classification; Anxiety Disorders; Somatoform Disorders; Dissociative Disorders; Mood Disorders; Schizophrenic Disorders; Personality Disorders; Psychopathology and the Law; Suicide; and Just for Fun.

General Resources in Abnormal Psychology

Psych Central—index, basic, short, links, graphics
Comprehensive site dedicated to mental health, has mailing lists, newsgroups, Web sites, book reviews, suicide help line, and much more. http://www.grohol.com/

Internet Mental Health—index, basic, short, links, graphics
Comprehensive page on mental health, has links to introduction, what's new, disorders, diagnosis, medications, magazine, Internet links, index, and more. http://www.mentalhealth.com/

PsychLink—index, basic, short, links, graphics, search
Page has a newsletter–style layout, with sections on news, continuing education, professional resources, databases, forums and discussions, and more. http://www.psychlink.com/

National Institute of Mental Health (NIMH)—index, basic, short, links, graphics, search
Home page of NIMH, has links to public information, news and events, grants and contracts, and research activities. http://www.nimh.nih.gov/

Teaching Clinical Psychology—index, basic, short, links, graphics
Site is devoted to the teaching of clinical psychology and has the following resources: in–class exercises, longer projects, course syllabi, books and manuals, links to other sites, and an index. http://www1.rider.edu/~suler/tcp.html

PsychScapes—index, basic, short, links, graphics, search
This page is for finding information and services in mental health: mental health workshops and conferences registry, therapist information network, speakers bureau, products and services notebook, publication previews, and more. http://www.mental-health.com/PsychScapes/home.html

InterPsych—index, interm., medium, links, graphics
Home page for a "cyberorganization," this page provides links to more than 40 forums on psychotherapeutic topics (from addiction to youth anxiety and depression); some forums require user to be a mental health professional. http://www.shef.ac.uk/~psysc/InterPsych/inter.html

Cyber–Psych—index, basic, short, links, graphics
Home page of a group that believes psychotherapy should also be provided on–line; links to information on a variety of psychological disorders and other information. http://www.webweaver.net/psych/

Mental Health Net—index, basic, short, links, graphics, search
Comprehensive site offers resources in disorders and treatments, professional resources, readings, managed care, news, and more. http://www.cmhc.com/

Mental Health Infosource—index, basic, short, links, graphics
Page has a link to a publication *Psychiatric Times* and other information on mental health, including disorders, MH interactive, other related resources, classifieds, and more. http://www.mhsource.com/

Perspectives—publication, interm., short, links, graphics, search
Home page of *Perspectives,* a magazine dedicated to mental health issues. Users may read articles and view back issues. http://www.cmhc.com/perspectives/

AABT—index, interm., short, links, graphics
Home page of the Association for Advancement of Behavior Therapy (AABT) contains links for About AABT, Publications, For the General Public, Related Sites, and others. http://server.psyc.vt.edu/aabt/

Behavior OnLine—index, basic, medium, links, graphics
Page contains a collection of basic resources for mental health professionals divided into the following categories: editiorial corner, ongoing discussions, organizations and interest groups, resources, and diversions. http://www.behavior.net/

Psychological Self–Help—book, basic, short, links, graphics, search
On–line version of book, *Psychological Self–Help,* contains 15 chapters on topics such as steps in self–help, depression, anger, dependency, and others. http://www.cmhc.com/psyhelp/

audioPsych—interactive, adv., short, links, audio
Users can earn continuing education credits (ceus) from this site using RealAudio technology. http://www.audiopsych.com/

Psychological Advisor Newsletter—interactive, basic, short, links, graphics, search
Interactive newsletter; users may send in their problems or comments, and editor will answer them on–line. http://www.psynews.com/

NetPsychology—index, interm., short, links, graphics, search
Home page that explores the delivery of psychological services via the Internet. http://netpsych.com/

Crisis, Grief, and Healing—index, basic, medium, links, graphics, search
Page is devoted to the attempt "to understand and honor the many different paths to heal strong emotions." Page has links to a variety of resources in healing, including excerpts from the book *Swallowed by a Snake.* http://www.webhealing.com/

National Alliance for the Mentally Ill (NAMI)—index, basic, short, links, graphics, search
Home page of the group has links to history of NAMI, press room, helpline, membership, related Web resources, and more. http://www.nami.org/

National Early Psychosis Project—index, basic, short, links, graphics
Page has information about early psychosis; links include newsletter, resource center, discussion forums, research projects and activities, and more. http://ariel.ucs.unimelb.EDU.AU:80/~nepp/

MadNation—index, basic, short, links, graphics
Home page for a group for "... people who experience mood swings, fears, voices and visions..." Includes Action, Madacademics, FAQ, Lists, Moments, and Writings. http://www.madnation.org/

The Effectiveness of Psychotherapy—article, interm., long, links, graphics
Full text of Martin Seligman's *American Psychologist* (1995) article on efficacy vs. effectiveness studies of psychotherapy, written in response to a *Consumer Reports* article on the efficacy of psychotherapy. http://www.cmhc.com/articles/seligm.htm

Models, Criteria, and Classification

The Ancients: Theories and Therapies for Psychopathology—tutorial, interm., long, links, graphics
Page discusses ancient approaches to psychopathology; includes demonological model, biological model, Plato's theories, and Aristotle's theories. http://library.scar.utoronto.ca/ClassicsC42/Fecteau/WEBPAGE/PSYCH.HTM

Being Sane in Insane Places—tutorial, interm., long, links
Page discusses Rosenhan's (1973) experiment, and speculates as to the definition of psychopathology. http://netra01.colchsfc.ac.uk/~psychlgy/rosenhan.htm

DSM–IV Questions and Answers—FAQ, interm., long, links, graphics
From the American Psychiatric Association, page answers common questions about the DSM–IV, the most used classification system of mental health problems in use today. http://www.psych.org/clin_res/q_a.html

ICD–9–CM—index, basic, short, links, graphics
Page has links to information about International Classification of Diseases, 9th revision, clinical modification (ICD–9–CM), another widely used system for classifying mental health problems. http://dumccss.mc.duke.edu/standards/HL7/termcode/icd9cm.htm

Clinical Psychology: Is the Future Back in Boulder?—article, interm., medium, links
> From on–line version of *Contemporary Psychology,* article is a retrospective review of Rotter's *Social Learning and Clinical Psychology.*
> http://www.apa.org/journals/cnt/may97/rotter.html

Mental Illness in America—text, interm., long, links, graphics
> From the National Institute of Mental Health (NIMH), discusses the prevalence and type of mental illness in America: the costs of mental illness and the savings from research, the diseases, from bench to bedside, and the future.
> http://www.nimh.nih.gov/research/amer.htm

Anxiety Disorders

Anxiety Disorders—index, basic, short, links, graphics
> From the Anxiety Disorders Association of America (ADAA), page has links to information about anxiety disorders for professionals and consumers.
> http://www.adaa.org/1a_doors/1a_01.htm

Anxiety Disorders in Children and Adolescents—article, interm., medium, links, graphics
> From *Contemporary Psychology* (1996), reviews *Anxiety Disorders in Children and Adolescents* (1995). Concludes that anxiety disorders are a significant source of trouble for many children and adolescents and that, contrary to popular belief, children do not simply grow out of them as a matter of course.
> http://www.apa.org/journals/march.html

The Phobia List—text, interm., long, links
> A comprehensive list of the names of phobias with a brief description of each. Page also provides for electronic submission of new names.
> http://www.sonic.net/~fredd/phobia1.html

Obsessive–Compulsive Disorder (OCD)—index, interm., short, links, graphics
> Page covers aspects of OCD, with links to abstracts, articles, medical information, definitions, and other resources. http://www.fairlite.com/ocd/

The Anxiety–Panic internet resource (tAPir)—index, basic, long, links, graphics
> Comprehensive site on anxiety and panic disorders: understanding anxiety, treatment, support, links to other related resources, and more.
> http://www.algy.com/anxiety/

On–line Screening for Anxiety—interactive, basic, short, links
> Test diagnoses anxiety, scores automatically.
> http://www.med.nyu.edu/Psych/screens/anx.html

Somatoform Disorders

Somatoform Disorder: How to Cope With It—FAQ, basic, short, links
> Answers four questions about somatoform disorder: what is somatoform disorder, what are the symptoms of somatoform disorder, what is the cause of somatoform disorder, and how is somatoform disorder treated.
> http://housecall.orbisnews.com/sponsors/aafp/topics/common/somato/page0.html

Somatization Disorder: Symptoms—text, basic, short, links, graphics
Describes the symptoms required to make a diagnosis of somatization disorder.
http://www.cmhc.com/disorders/sx94.htm

Somatization Disorder—text, interm., medium, links
Linked page covers issues in somatization disorder: definition, causes, incidence, risk factors, prevention, symptoms, treatment, prognosis, and complications.
http://housecall.orbisnews.com/databases/ami/convert/000955.html

Conversion Disorder: Symptoms—text, basic, short, links, graphics
Describes the symptoms required to make a diagnosis of conversion disorder.
http://www.cmhc.com/disorders/sx43.htm

Conversion Disorder—text, interm., medium, links
Linked page covers issues in conversion disorder: definition, causes, incidence, and risk factors, prevention, symptoms, treatment, prognosis, and complications.
http://housecall.orbisnews.com/databases/ami/convert/000954.html

Hypochondriasis: Symptoms—text, basic, short, links, graphics
Describes the symptoms required to make a diagnosis of hypochondriasis.
http://www.cmhc.com/disorders/sx57.htm

Hypochondriasis—text, interm., medium, links
Linked page covers issues in hypochondriasis: definition, causes, incidence, risk factors, prevention, symptoms, treatment, prognosis, and complications.
http://housecall.orbisnews.com/databases/ami/convert/001236.html

Dissociative Disorders

Dissociative Amnesia: Symptoms—text, basic, short, links, graphics
Describes the symptoms required to make a diagnosis of dissociative amnesia.
http://www.cmhc.com/disorders/sx46.htm

Dissociative Fugue: Symptoms—text, basic, short, links, graphics
Describes the symptoms required to make a diagnosis of dissociative fugue.
http://www.cmhc.com/disorders/sx87.htm

Treatment of Multiple Personality Disorder—text, adv., long, links, graphics
Linked page discusses multiple personality disorder or dissociative identity disorder: the 3–P model of MPD, dissociation and MPD, communicating with each personality state, developing interpersonality communication, the need to hospitalize, medications, and more.
http://www.dhearts.org/libraries/read/treatmpd.html

Treatment of Multiple Personality Disorder—text, adv., long, links
Comprehensive article on treatment of MPD includes eclectically oriented treatment programs, adjuncts and other therapeutic approaches, iatrogenic concerns, conclusions, and references.
http://www.auburn.edu/~mcquedr/psyinfo/mpd.htm

Legitimacy of Multiple Personality Disorder—text, interm., medium, links, graphics

Page discusses book *Multiple Identities and False Memories: A Sociocognitive Perspective* by the late Nicholas Spanos argues that MPD is a "social construction," not a real psychopathology. http://www.apa.org/releases/book.html

Multiple Personality Disorder (Dissociative Identity Disorder)—text, adv., long, links

An analysis critical of the diagnosis of MPD by Paul R. McHugh argues that MPD is "created by therapists." http://www.psycom.net/mchugh.html

Dissociation and Multiple Personality Disorder—index, basic, short, links, graphics

Page contains writing by sufferers of MPD and links to related resources. http://fly.hiwaay.net:8000/~garson/dissoc.htm

Definition of Multiple Personality Disorder—text, adv., long, links, graphics

Ralph Allison discusses history of diagnosis of MPD, and argues for the reality of the diagnosis. http://www.dissociation.com/index/definition/

Mood Disorders

A Guide to Depressive and Manic Depressive Illness—text, basic, long, links

From the National Depressive and Manic Depressive Association (NDMDA); provides complete linked overview of mood disorders: introduction to affective disorders, symptoms of depression and mania, treatment options, and much more. http://www.ndmda.org/ID.HTM

Depression Central—index, basic, long, links, graphics

Self–described clearinghouse for depressive disorders and treatments: causes of mood disorders, classification of mood disorders, bipolar disorder, suicide and suicide prevention, and much more. http://www.psycom.net/depression.central.html

Major Depressive Disorder: Treatment—text, interm., long, links, graphics

Discusses treatment options for major depression: what therapy is best, psychosocial therapies, medical therapies, and references. http://www.mentalhealth.com/dis/p20-md01.html

Women and Depression—text, basic, long, links, graphics

From APA, contains questions and answers to questions about depression and women. http://www.apa.org/pubinfo/depress.html

Information About Bipolar Disorder and Manic Depression—index, basic, short, links, graphics

Provides basic information about bipolar disorder grouped in four headings: general information, diagnosis, treatment, and miscellaneous. Includes links to FAQ on bipolar disorder, American and European descriptions, articles about bipolar disorder, and writing by patients. http://www.pendulum.org/info.htm

Bipolar Disorder: Symptoms—text, basic, short, links, graphics
Describes the symptoms required to make a diagnosis of bipolar disorder.
http://www.cmhc.com/disorders/sx20.htm

Seasonal Affective Disorder—text, basic, long, links, graphics
Discusses the diagnosis of seasonal affective disorder (SAD), a mild depressive
condition that affects many people in the fall and winter.
http://mentalhealth.miningco.com/library/weekly/aa120897.htm

On–line Depression Screening Test—interactive, basic, short, links
Test diagnoses depression, scores automatically.
http://www.med.nyu.edu/Psych/screens/depres.html

Schizophrenic Disorders

Schizophrenia: Symptoms—text, interm., long, links, graphics
Describes the symptoms required to make a diagnosis of schizophrenia.
http://www.cmhc.com/disorders/sx31.htm

Schizophrenia—text, interm., long, links
Linked page covers issues in schizophrenia: definition, causes, incidence, risk
factors, prevention, symptoms, treatment, prognosis, and complications.
http://www.healthanswers.com/database/ami/converted/000928.html

Health Guide: Schizophrenia—index, basic, short, links, graphics, search
Comprehensive page on schizophrenia: what is schizophrenia, causes of
schizophrenia, symptoms of schizophrenia, related disorders, treatment, living
with schizophrenia, and working with health care professionals.
http://www.healthguide.com/Schiz/default.htm

Schizophrenia—tutorial, basic, long, links, graphics
General information on schizophrenia and its treatment: criteria, definition,
psychotic disorders, treatment (psychotherapy), treatment (pharmacotherapy),
schizophrenia subtypes, schizophrenia diagnosis flow chart.
http://www.psyweb.com/Mdisord/schid.html

Understanding Schizophrenia—tutorial, basic, long, links, graphics
Comprehensive look at schizophrenia: what is schizophrenia, who gets
schizophrenia, what are the symptoms of schizophrenia, how is schizophrenia
diagnosed, how is schizophrenia treated, and more.
http://www.mhsource.com/advocacy/narsad/schiz.html

The Etiology of Schizophrenia—interactive, interm., short, links, graphics
From EXPERSIM, users may set values for variables related to schizophrenia and
then "run" an experiment on those variables and interpret the results.
http://samiam.colorado.edu/~mcclella/expersim/introschizophrenia.html

The Schizophrenia Home Page—index, basic, short, links, graphics
Page is dedicated to the memory of patient who took his own life, is run by that
patient's brother. Page provides e–mail updates about schizophrenia, chat rooms,
information for families of patients, and more. http://www.schizophrenia.com/

Studies of Schizophrenia—index, adv., short, links, graphics
Home page of the Mental Health Clinical Research Center (MH–CRC) which specializes in research on schizophrenia. Current areas of study are diagnosis and phenomenology, magnetic resonance imaging, positron emission tomography, cognitive neuroscience, clinical neuropharmacology, and genetics/epidemiology. http://data-entry.psychiatry.uiowa.edu/mhcrc/

How to Manage 5 Common Symptoms of Schizophrenia—article, basic, long, links
Linked article abbreviated for popular use; original appeared in *Hospital and Community Psychiatry* (1997). Describes five common symptoms of schizophrenia and gives advice on how to manage them: paranoia, denial of illness, stigma, demoralization, and terror of being psychotic. http://www.schizophrenia.com/ami/coping/symptom.html

Personality Disorders

Personality Disorders—index, basic, short, links, graphics, search
Comprehensive page on personality disorders: what are personality disorders, the three major classifications, what causes personality disorders, treatment, and resources. http://www.healthguide.com/Personality/default.htm

Personality Disorders—index, basic, short, links, graphics
Introduces the diagnosis of the personality disorders: symptoms, treatment, on–line resources, organizations, and on–line support. http://personalitydisorders.cmhc.com/

Antisocial Personality Disorder—index, basic, short, links, graphics
Site links to information on antisocial personality disorder: description, diagnosis, treatment, magazine articles, and links to related sites. http://www.mentalhealth.com/dis/p20-pe04.html

Avoidant Personality Disorder: Symptoms—text, basic, short, links, graphics
Describes the symptoms required to make a diagnosis of avoidant personality disorder. http://www.cmhcsys.com/disorders/sx8.htm

Borderline Personality Disorder—index, basic, short, links, graphics
Site links to information on borderline personality disorder (BPD): description, diagnosis, treatment, magazine articles, and links to related sites. http://www.mentalhealth.com/dis/p20-pe05.html

Borderline Personality Disorder Central—index, basic, short, links, graphics
Site covers Borderline Personality Disorder and has links to help identify individuals with BPD, a FAQ, a new book on BPD, and to other related links. http://member.aol.com/BPDCentral/index.html

Dependent Personality Disorder—index, basic, short, links, graphics
Site links to information on dependent personality disorder: description, diagnosis, treatment, magazine articles, and links to related sites. http://www.mentalhealth.com/dis/p20-pe09.html

Histrionic Personality Disorder—index, basic, short, links, graphics
Site links to information on histrionic personality disorder: description, diagnosis, treatment, magazine articles, and links to related sites.
http://www.mentalhealth.com/dis/p20-pe06.html

Narcissistic Personality Disorder: Symptoms—text, basic, short, links, graphics
Describes the symptoms required to make a diagnosis of narcissistic personality disorder. http://www.cmhcsys.com/disorders/sx36.htm

Obsessive–Compulsive Disorder: Symptoms—text, basic, short, links, graphics
Describes the symptoms required to make a diagnosis of obsessive–compulsive personality disorder. http://www.cmhcsys.com/disorders/sx26.htm

Paranoid Personality Disorder: Symptoms—text, basic, short, links, graphics
Describes the symptoms required to make a diagnosis of paranoid personality disorder. http://www.cmhc.com/disorders/sx37.htm

Schizoid Personality Disorder—index, basic, short, links, graphics
Site links to information on schizoid personality disorder: description, diagnosis, treatment, magazine articles, and links to related sites.
http://www.mentalhealth.com/dis/p20-pe02.html

Schizotypal Personality Disorder—index, basic, short, links, graphics
Site links to information on schizotypal personality disorder: description, diagnosis, treatment, magazine articles, and links to related sites.
http://www.mentalhealth.com/dis/p20-pe03.html

Psychopathology and the Law

The Insanity Defense—FAQ, basic, long, links, graphics
From the American Psychiatric Association, answers questions about the insanity defense. http://www.psych.org/public_info/INSANI~1.HTM

Combating Workplace Violence—tutorial, basic, short, links, graphics
From the Illinois State Police, discusses identification and prevention of workplace violence. http://www.state.il.us/ISP/viowkplc/vwphome.htm

Let's Stop Being Nutty About the Mentally Ill—article, basic, long, links, graphics
From *City Journal* and written by E. Fuller Torrey; argues that deinstitutionalization of severely mentally ill patients was a mistake.
http://www.manhattan-institute.org/html/7_3_a2.htm

Suicide

American Foundation for Suicide Prevention (AFSP)—index, basic, short, links, graphics
Home page of the AFSP has links to research, depression and suicide, suicide support, assisted suicide, neurobiology and suicide, suicide and AIDS, youth suicide, suicide facts, and more. http://www.afsp.org/

Suicide Prevention Quiz—interactive, basic, short, links, graphics
Page presents 13 statements about suicide that users can then click on to see if the statement was true or false. http://www.sfsuicide.org/quiz.html

Is Assisted Suicide Ever a Rational Choice?—article, basic, long, links, graphics, search
From the APA's *Monitor* (1997), examines the issues surrounding assisted suicide. http://www.apa.org/monitor/apr97/suicide.html

Chronology of Events Related to Assisted Suicide—text, interm., long, links, graphics
From the Michigan Right to Life chapter, provides list of historical and recent events in the right to die movement. http://www.rtl.org/lbpchron.htm

Just for Fun

Dr. Katz, Professional Therapist—index, basic, short, links, graphics
Comedy Central's cartoon character, Dr. Katz, professional therapist, has his own home page. Users may select from: See the Doctor, Dr. Katz's Day Planner, Patient Files, or Dear Dr. Katz. Page also links to show schedule, the comic strip, and to RealVideo gallery (requires RealPlayer). http://www.comcentral.com/katz/index.html

Therapy

The treatment of those with psychological problems has always been an issue in society. Long before psychology, such people were treated in a variety of ways, both humanely and otherwise. Freud and his psychodynamic theories popularized insight therapies. By the 1930s, the terms from the psychodynamic model were well known to the general public. The use of electroconvulsive therapy and, later, the discovery of chemical agents to treat depression and schizophrenia led to advances in treatment but also changed the infrastructure of therapy, leading to deinstitutionalization. Behavioral therapies, derived from learning theory and conditioning, became popular because they addressed behavioral change successfully. The URLs are grouped by the categories of: General Resources in Therapy; Insight Therapies; Behavior Therapies; Biomedical Therapies; and History of Therapy.

General Resources in Therapy

Theories and Approaches in Psychotherapy—index, basic, short, links, graphics
Covers the following approaches: Adlerian, Gestalt, client–centered, psychoanalytic, Jungian, cognitive behavior, existential, reality, behavior, and transactional analysis. http://www.gallaudet.edu/~11mgourn/

How to Choose a Psychologist—text, basic, long, links, graphics
From APA, provides advice on how to choose a psychotherapist.
http://www.apa.org/pubinfo/howto.html

Types of Therapies—text, interm., long, links, graphics
Describes four different approaches to therapy: psychodynamic, cognitive–behavioral, humanistic (existential), and eclectic.
http://www.grohol.com/therapy.htm

Glossary of Mental Health Terms—index, basic, short, links, graphics, search
Page allows user to see definitions of commonly used terms in mental health.
http://mirconnect.com/glossary/index.html

Therapy FAQ—FAQ, basic, short, links, graphics
Answers 13 common questions about therapy: why go to a therapist, what kind of therapist do I choose, when should I end therapy, and more.
http://abulafia.st.hmc.edu/~mmiles/faq.html

Disorders and Treatment—index, basic, long, links, graphics
Page consists of a comprehensive list of disorders and their treatments.
http://www.cmhc.com/disorders/

Group Psychotherapy for the Layman—text, basic, medium, links, graphics
Linked text page describes and discusses group psychotherapy: how does it work, who can benefit from group psychotherapy, what is expected from the participant, and more. http://freud.tau.ac.il/~haimw/group1.html

American Dance Therapy Association (ADTA)—index, basic, short, links, graphics
Home page of the ADTA, includes links to FAQ and other related sites. http://www.citi.net/ADTA/

Marriage and Family Therapy—index, interm., long, links, graphics
Provides links to resources in marriage and family therapy: Web resources, newsgroups, mailing lists, journals, and professional organizations and centers. http://www.cmhc.com/guide/pro06.htm

Primal Psychotherapy—index, interm., long, links, graphics, search
Comprehensive page on primal therapy; includes a wide variety of information and links to resources.
http://www.net-connect.net/~jspeyrer/primal1.htm

Liberation Psychotherapy—index, interm., medium, links, graphics
Home page of two transactional analysts promotes their approach to treating problems with parents, trauma, values, and guilt and shame. http://liberationpsych.org/

Narrative Therapy—text, interm. medium, links, graphics
Page describes narrative therapy, an approach that "...focuses on externalizing problems." http://onthenet.com.au/~pict/mentnarr.htm

Treatment of Drug Abuse and Addiction—text, basic, long, links, graphics
Linked text page covers basic topics in the treatment of drug abuse: undoing the addiction, changing behavior, is it a disease, and more. http://www.mentalhealth.com/mag1/p5h-sb04.html

Multicultural Counseling and Psychotherapy Survey—interactive, interm., medium, links, graphics
Users may respond to 20–item survey on personal values which attempts to determine the source of those values.
http://www.yorku.ca./faculty/academic/pwaxer/multi.htm

On–line Dictionary of Mental Health—index, interm., short, links, graphics, search
Comprehensive dictionary of mental health topics. Users may search alphabetically or via internal search.
http://www.shef.ac.uk/~psysc/psychotherapy/index.html

Web Psychologist—interactive, basic, long, links, graphics
Users may select from a number of typical scenarios in which counseling might be effective to see what advice was given. Scenarios include: depressed, alone, sensitive, fear of love, arachnophobia, and more.
http://www.queendom.com/shrink.html

Dr. Magoo's Office—index, basic, short, links, graphics
Page has six links to childhood behavioral problems (anxiety disorders, behavioral disorders, developmental problems, disorders of physical functioning, psychotic disorders, and other problems). Clicking on the problem reveals a linked list of cases. Clicking on each case reveals therapies for that case.
http://tuweb.ucis.dal.ca/~drmagoo/intro.htm

Insight Therapies

Psychoanalysis Adapts to the 1990s—article, interm., medium, links, graphics
From APA's *Monitor* (1996), discusses changes in the practice of psychoanalysis: more psychologists as analysts, changing treatment directions,and more.
http://www.apa.org/monitor/sep96/modern.html

Freud, Jung, and Psychoanalysis—article, adv., long, links
A detailed look at the relationship between Freud and Jung.
http://uslink.net/ddavis/jungfreu.html

Freud's Free Association and Writing—text, basic, short, links
Describes Freud's technique of free association and how free association derived from a writing technique published during his time.
http://www.utoledo.edu/homepages/ddavis/freudfre.htm

Hypnosis and Catharsis—text, basic, short, links, graphics
Discusses Freud's early use of hypnosis in therapy and his discovery of catharsis.
http://www.stg.brown.edu/projects/hypertext/landow/HTatBrown/freud
/Hypnosis_Catharsis.html

Free Association—text, basic, short, links, graphics
Short overview of Freud's switch to free association instead of hypnosis; also mentions the consequent discovery of repression.
http://www.stg.brown.edu/projects/hypertext/landow/HTatBrown/freud
/Free_Association.html

Psychoanalytic Resources—index, basic, medium, links, graphics
Page on modern psychoanalysis, contains links to: FAQ, Jung, Klein, Lacan, Laing, miscellaneous resources and institutes, and more.
http://www.umdnj.edu/psyevnts/psa.html

Where Will Psychoanalysis Survive?—article, adv., long, links, graphics
From *Harvard Magazine* (1997), a long look at the future of psychoanalysis.
http://www.harvard-magazine.com/jf97/freud.html

Gestalt Therapy—index, basic, short, links, graphics
Home page sponsored by the *Gestalt Journal* and the International Gestalt Therapy Association provides links for finding therapists and to materials on Gestalt therapy. http://www.gestalt.org/index.htm

Child/Adolescent Psychoanalysis and Psychotherapy—text, interm., medium, links
Advice to parents about when to seek therapy for children and adolescents.
http://www.westnet.com/~pbrand/

Client–Centered Therapy—index, basic, medium, links, graphics
Page covers Rogerian client–centered therapy, with short definition of technique and links to glossary, history of Carl Rogers, and other links on this type of therapy. http://www.gallaudet.edu/~11mgourn/client.html

Still Relevant–Still Revolutionary—article, adv., long, links, graphics
From *Contemporary Psychology,* reviews three of Carl Roger's books and concludes that Roger's work is still revolutionary 40 years later.
http://www.apa.org/journals/patterso.html

Behavior Therapies

What is Cognitive Behavioral Therapy?—text, basic, medium, links, graphics
Provides description and definition of the technique of cognitive–behavioral therapy. http://pages.nyu.edu/~lqh6007/BehavioralAssociates/therapy.html

Basics of Cognitive Therapy—text, basic, medium, links, graphics
Linked text page on cognitive therapy: what is cognitive therapy, what is the research background of cognitive therapy, how is cognitive therapy conducted, how can I learn more about cognitive therapy, and suggested readings.
http://mindstreet.com/cbt.html

Cognitive Behavior Group Therapy—text, interm. long, links
Page discusses the basic principles of cognitive behavior therapy: cognitive theory, step 1: elicit automatic thoughts, step 2: identify underlying irrational beliefs, step 3: challenge the irrational beliefs, and step 4: replace the irrational beliefs.
http://www.pacificcoast.net/~aegis/prin_cb1.htm

Albert Ellis Institute—index, basic, medium, links, graphics
Home page of the Albert Ellis Institute, a center for rational–emotive therapy. Site contains information about the Institute, questions and answers about rational–emotive therapy, call for research participation, on–line pamphlets, and more. http://www.IRET.org/

Coping With Disabilities the Albert Ellis Way—article, interm., medium, links, graphics
From APA's *Monitor* (1995), describes how Albert Ellis, founder of rational–emotive behavior therapy, uses his own techniques to cope with his own disabilities. http://www.apa.org/monitor/oct95/ellis.html

Passionate Skeptic and Relentless Healer—article, interm., medium, links, graphics
From *Contemporary Psychology* (1996), reviews the book, *Albert Ellis–Passionate Skeptic* (1988). Discusses Ellis's life and the development of rational–emotional behavior therapy. http://www.apa.org/journals/wiener.html

Behavior Therapy—index, basic, short, links, graphics
Page covers behavior therapy, has short definition of technique and links to glossary and other links on this type of therapy.
http://www.gallaudet.edu/~11mgourn/bt.html

Behavior Therapy: Key Concepts—text, basic, short, links
Lists the principles involved in the "Basic ID" acronym of behavior therapy.
http://www.primenet.com/~dannell/andy/psych/personality/kcbehave.html

Joseph Wolpe—text, basic, short, links, graphics
Short biography of the developer of desensitization, or counterconditioning.
http://psy1.clarion.edu/jms/Wolpe.html

Sexual Aversion Therapy—text, basic, short, links, graphics
Short description of the technique of sexual aversion therapy.
http://www.pathfinder.com/altculture/aentries_ew/s/sexualxave.html

A *Clockwork Orange*—index, interm., medium, links, graphics
The information about the movie and novel of the same title. Alex, the violent hero, is converted to a scared shell of his former self through aversive therapy.
http://www.tu-harburg.de/rzt/rzt/it/film3.html

Biofeedback—text, basic, short, links, graphics
Provides basic information on biofeedback and its use in therapy.
http://pages.nyu.edu/~lqh6007/BehavioralAssociates/biofeedback.html

Association for Applied Psychophysiology and Biofeedback (AAPB)—index, basic, short, links, graphics
Home page of the AAPB, has links about AAPB, what is biofeedback, new research, news, media catalog, meetings and workshops, conference center, and other sites. http://www.aapb.org/

Biomedical Therapies

Ask Noah About: Mental Health—index, interm., long, links, graphics
Page provides advice on how to deal with a wide variety of mental health issues, including suicide prevention, medications and side effects, tests, exams, procedures, and more.
http://www.noah.cuny.edu/mentalhealth/mental.html

Psychotherapeutic Drugs—tutorial, interm., long, links
Discusses psychoactive drugs used in therapy: antidepressants, anxiolytics, antipsychotics, antimanics, sedatives and hypnotics, drugs used to treat side effects of other drugs, and drugs used for hyperactivity.
http://www.onlinepsych.com/treat/drugs.htm

Panic and Anxiety Disorder Medications—index, basic, short, links, graphics, search
Information on the following drugs: benzodiazepines, selective serotonin reuptake inhibitors, tricyclic antidepressants, monoamine oxidase inhibitors, other antidepressants, and other medications used for anxiety disorders.
http://panicdisorder.miningco.com/msub5d.htm

Anxiety—text, basic, medium, links, graphics
Discusses anxiety symptoms and their treatment via drugs.
http://www.geisinger.edu/ghs/pubtips/A/Anxiety.htm

Antianxiety Agents—index, interm., medium, links, graphics
Covers the properties of Valium, Vistaril, and Xanax.
http://www.dentaldigest.com/prescrip/anxiety.html

Benzodiazepines—FAQ, basic, long, links
Answers questions about the major tranquilizers in the benzodiazepine group (Thorazine, Mellaril, Haldol, and others).
http://www.schizophrenia.com/ami/meds/benzo.html

Chlorpromazine—text, interm., short, links, graphics
Basic information on chlorpromazine, a commonly used phenothiazine (Thorazine), used in the treatment of schizophrenia .
http://www.avm.com.au/agtm/drugprofiles/chlorpromazine.html

Electroconvulsive Therapy—FAQ, basic, medium, links, graphics
From the American Psychiatric Association, answers basic questions about electroconvulsive therapy. http://www.psych.org/public_info/ECT~1.HTM

Electroconvulsive Therapy—text, basic, short, links, graphics
From the National Mental Health Association, discusses the pros and cons of electroconvulsive therapy. http://www.nmha.org/info/factsheets/62.html

Electroconvulsive Therapy—index, basic, medium, links, graphics
Provides basic information about electroconvulsive therapy: definition, reason for the procedure, preparation, procedure, and side effects.
http://www.noah.cuny.edu/illness/mentalhealth/cornell/tests/ect.html

History of Therapy

Witchcraft in Early Modern Europe and America—biblio., adv., long, links
Comprehensive bibliography of sources on witchcraft. In the Middle Ages and beyond, those with psychological problems were often labelled as witches.
http://www.hist.unt.edu/witch01a.htm

Malleus Malificarum—book, adv., long, links, graphics
Contains substantial portion in English translation of the book of the same title used to identify and condemn witches (the insane) during the Middle Ages and beyond. http://www.klammeraffe.org/~brandy/hexen/MalleusMalificarum/

Landmarks in Psychology—graphic, interm., short, links, graphics
Page contains graphics of original depictions of landmark events in the history of treatment. Includes Pinel unlocking the inmates of Bicetre, Mesmer (portrait), Pavlov and his coworkers, Freud and his associates, and John B. Watson (portrait). Also has links to other related sites on treatment.
http://www.alaska.net/~enigma/psychsoc/landmark.htm

Chronic Care in America—index, interm., short, links, graphics
Comprehensive set of articles sponsored by Robert Wood Johnson Foundation; includes fact sheets and graphs. Articles are categorized as follows: introduction to chronic conditions, the chronic care system, stresses in the system, and others.
http://www.rwjf.org/library/chrcare/contents.htm

The Madness of Deinstitutionalization—article, basic, long, links
   From *Wall Street Journal* (1996), attacks the practice of deinstitutionalization as
   financially wasteful and therapeutically ineffective.
   http://www.psych-health.com/madness.htm

Stress, Coping, and Health

One of the most useful applications of psychology is in the area of stress management and healthy living. So much of life can be positively enhanced by successful strategies of dealing with stress and by prevention. Stress cannot be eliminated from life, but its effects can be recognized and dealt with. Eliminating risky behaviors and promoting healthy ones can also enhance the quality of life. Dealing with illness is another area in which psychology can help those afflicted, as well as relatives and friends of the afflicted. The URLs are grouped by the categories of: General Resources in Stress, Coping, and Health; Types of Stress; Responses to Stress; Risky Behaviors; Better Health and Prevention; Coping With Illness; and Just for Fun.

General Resources in Stress, Coping, and Health

Stress: Causes and Effects—index, basic, short, links, graphics
Comprehensive page on stress: overview, questionnaires, management, and summary. Questionnaires include: life change, life style, work stress, and burnout. http://www.cardinalpoints.com/stress/00stress.html

America's Best Hospitals (1997)—index, basic, short, links, graphics
From *US News,* page provides links to the cover story, rankings, related stories, rankings by disease specialty, and more. http://www4.usnews.com/usnews/nycu/hosphigh.htm

Virtual Reality in Medicine Lab—index, basic, short, links, graphics
Page provides links to three demonstrations of virtual reality technology in medicine: the virtual ear, 3–D radiologic image data, and computer–aided design and fabrication of cranial implants. http://www2.sbhis.uic.edu/VRML/

CPI Calculation Machine—interactive, basic, short, links, graphics
Users may obtain rate of inflation between any two years (limited to the years 1913–1997). Money and its loss of value over time is a major source of stress. http://woodrow.mpls.frb.fed.us/economy/calc/cpihome.html

Complete Home Medical Guide—index, basic, short, links, graphics
From the Columbia University College of Physicians and Surgeons, this site provides medical advice of all kinds: using our health system, new approaches to wellness, symptoms and diagnoses, first aid and safety, treatment and prevention of disease, drugs and their uses, and four appendices. http://cpmcnet.columbia.edu/texts/guide/

Society of Behavioral Medicine—index, basic, medium, links, graphics
Home page of the society contains links to announcements, behavioral medicine resources, publications, membership information, and more. http://socbehmed.org/sbm/sbm.htm

MEdIC—index, interm., short, links, graphics
From the University of Texas–Houston Department of Pathology and Laboratory Medicine, its medical instructional multimedia tool, includes: health explorer, education, professional, and others. "We believe computerized self–instructional multimedia learning is an effective educational tool. This concept forms the basis of the MEdIC concept as applied to health information."
http://medic.med.uth.tmc.edu/index.html

Blonz Guide to Nutrition, Food, and Health Resources—index, basic, medium, links, graphics, search
Comprehensive page has a variety of links for topics in health, including nutrition, food and fitness, food, health and medical, and many more.
http://www.wenet.net/blonz/

Types of Stress

The Different Kinds of Stress—tutorial, basic, medium, links, graphics
From APA, discusses three types of stress: acute, acute episodic, and chronic. Offers advice on how to deal with each type. http://helping.apa.org/stress4.html

Stress—index, basic, short, links, graphics, search
Page provides general information on stress, including: what is stress, control and stress, maintaining a healthy lifestyle, and more.
http://healthguide.com/Stress/default.htm

Stress—text, basic, medium, links, graphics
Page describes stress, its effects, and how to cope with it. Sections include: what is stress, what causes stress, when is it a problem, recognizing it, and avoiding it. http://www.rtc-carlow.ie/SUHome/stress.html

Stress, Anxiety, Fears, and Psychosomatic Disorders—index, basic, short, links, graphics
Comprehensive page on stress and other related disorders: signs of stress, sources and types of stress, theories explaining stress and anxiety, ways of handling stress and anxiety, and treatment of specific anxiety–based problems.
http://www.cmhc.com/psyhelp/chap5/

Sources and Types of Stress—text, basic, long, links, graphics
The types of conflict that cause stress (i.e., approach–avoidance and others), the general adaptation syndrome, the long–term effects of stress, and other related topics. http://www.cmhc.com/psyhelp/chap5/chap5d.htm

Stress Test—interactive, basic, short
Copy of Holmes and Rahe's (1967) Life Changes questionnaire. Users must add up the Life Change Units (LCUs) themselves. http://www.prcn.org/next/stress.html

Responses to Stress

Learned Helplessness—text, basic, short, links, graphics, search
Outlines the traits and attributions of learned helplessness.
http://healthguide.com/Stress/helpless.htm

Stress Manangement: Review of Principles—index, basic, short, links, graphics
Page links to articles and sound clips on stress management. Articles include: conceptual understanding of stressors and stress responses, personality, perception and sources of stress (sound clip), psychophysiology of stress and relaxation (sound clip), lifestyle behavior patterns and the stress response, cognitive and behavioral interventions (sound clip), measurement of stress reactions and relaxation responses, and others. http://www.unl.edu/stress/mgmt/

Is Your Stress IQ Hurting Your Performance?—interactive, basic, short, links, graphics
Users may answer a short questionnaire (with attached answer key) designed to assess whether or not stress is interfering with their athletic performance. http://cybertowers.com/selfhelp/articles/sports/spstress.html

Job Burnout Test—interactive, basic, short, links
Users may take a 20–item questionnaire on job burnout. An assessment of the user's level of burnout is provided via the Web. http://www.ventura.com/jsearch/unique/12781/jshome2b.html

Posttraumatic Stress Disorder (PTSD) Symptoms—text, basic, medium, links, graphics, search
Page describes the symptoms of PTSD in detail. http://www.cmhcsys.com/disorders/sx32.htm

Type A Behavior—text, basic, short, links, graphics
Describes Type A Behavior Pattern (TABP); links to on–line test and related sites. http://www.msnbc.com/onair/nbc/nightlynews/stress/default.asp

Type A Behavior Quiz—interactive, basic, short, links, graphics
Users may take a short quiz to determine if they are Type A. Users must score the quiz themselves. http://www.msnbc.com/onair/nbc/nightlynews/stress/stresstypea.asp

Type A Behavior—text, interm., long, links, graphics
Describes the symptomology of Type A Behavior Pattern (TABP): what is TABP, TABP and job stress, how to measure TABP, TABP and coronary heart disease, conclusions, and references. http://www.workhealth.org/risk/rfbtypea.htm

The Humor Project Inc.—index, basic, short, links, graphics
Home page of an organization dedicated to tapping the positive power of humor and creativity: Daily Affirmation, Chicken Soup, *Laughing Matters Magazine*, Book Store, and other links. http://www.wizvax.net/humor/

Health and Quality of Life On–line Questionnaires—interactive, basic, long, links, graphics
Users may answer questions about their diet and lifestyle. Results are provided. The questionnaire is part of a study on diet and lifestyle. http://salmon.psy.plym.ac.uk/research/hyland/health.html

Psychosomatic Illness—text, basic, short, links, graphics, search
Page contains short definition of psychosomatic illness and links to related topics. http://www.med.umich.edu/1libr/mental/psysom01.htm

Risky Behaviors

How to Quit Smoking—text, basic, long, links, graphics
Page provides a time–based set of hints for quitting smoking.
http://www.nothinbut.net/~tom-m/nosmoke.html

Drug and Alcohol Addiction—text, basic, long
Introduction to the process of addiction, page lists orientations, outcomes, and conclusions; includes a bibliography.
http://www2.one.net.au/~allen/academic/alcohol.htm

Armed Robbery Page—index, basic, short, links, graphics, Java
Designed to prepare businesses and employees in high–risk situations, this page provides links designed to help minimize those risks. Links include a survey, perspectives on becoming a witness, resisting a holdup, and others.
http://www.ior.com/~jdmoore/

The First 500,000 AIDS Cases—index, basic, short, links, graphics
Changes in AIDS patterns between 1981 and 1995 with a series of graphs.
http://topchoice.com/~psyche/aids95us.html

Preventing HIV Infection—tutorial, basic, long, links, graphics
Page provides advice on how to prevent HIV infection: what are HIV and AIDS, how is HIV passed on, who has HIV, HIV and sex, safer drug use, HIV and health care, HIV and pregnancy, and towards the future.
http://www.tht.org.uk/prvinfec.htm

Better Health and Prevention

Preventive Health Center—index, basic, short, links, graphics
General page on ways people can maintain their health and prevent disease includes sections on nutrition, smoking, heart disease, vision, stress management, depression, and more. http://www.md-phc.com/index.html

Fitness Link—index, basic, short, links, graphics, Java
Comprehensive page on fitness and health: features, mind–body, nutrition, exercise, and more. Page also has links to related sites.
http://www.fitnesslink.com/

Men's Health—publication, basic, short, links, graphics, search
On–line magazine devoted to men's health. http://www.menshealth.com/

Women's Health Weekly—publication, basic, short, links, graphics, search
On–line magazine devoted to women's health.
http://www.newsfile.com/homepage/1w.htm

Breast Cancer Information Clearinghouse—index, basic, short, links, graphics
Page provides links to information on breast cancer and support for its victims.
http://nysernet.org/bcic/

Coping with Illness

Healthfinder Guided Tour–Cancer—FAQ, basic, long, links, graphics
From the U.S. government, this page answers questions about cancer and has links to other related sites. http://www.healthfinder.gov/tours/cancer.htm

HealthyWay—index, basic, short, links, graphics
A Canadian set of pages on health, nutrition, and other topics: addictions, disabilities, healthy eating, oral health, sex and sexuality, sports and fitness, and much more. http://www.mb.sympatico.ca/Contents/Health/health.html

Health Direct—index, basic, short, links, graphics
A large site covering health issues. Page is arranged in four sections: health news, health check, health care, and health direct.
http://www.healthdirect.com/home.htm

Alzheimer's Association—index, basic, short, links, graphics
Home page of Alzheimer's Association has links to About Us, In the News, Caregiver Resources, Research and Medical, Public Policy, and more.
http://www.alz.org/

The Trauma Foundation—index, basic, short, links, graphics, search
Home page of advocacy group dedicated to minimizing trauma injuries and deaths. Page includes: alert, what's new, in the news, alcohol, injuries, and library.
http://www.traumafdn.org/index.html

Just for Fun

Irritation, Aggravation, and Frustration—text, basic, short, links, graphics
Classic joke about the differences among the three.
http://www.genius.net/indolink/youth/mazza/alf.html

17

Social Behavior

The study of people in groups, social psychology, is a major subfield of psychology. Social psychologists study a wide variety of behaviors in social settings. How people size each other up, how behavior is explained to oneself, and how people get along in groups are all examples of social psychology. The relationship between attitudes and behavior is another area of long–standing interest. Milgram's research in conformity and obedience inspired continuing study and showed the need for ethical constraints on research. Faulty decision making by groups also led to research in group processes in that and other related areas. Finally, the problems of prejudice have long interested social psychologists. The URLs are grouped by the categories of: General Resources in Social Behavior; Impressions of Others; Attributions; Relationships; Attitudes; Conformity and Obedience; Group Processes; Prejudice; and Just for Fun.

General Resources in Social Behavior

Social Psychology Network—index, basic, short, links
An award–winning site for social psychology includes links to social psychology topics, graduate work in social psychology, home pages of social psychologists, on–line studies, textbooks, and more. http://www.wesleyan.edu/spn/

Psychology Web Archive—index, basic, short, links, graphics
Page contains links to resources in social psychology: articles, references, software, and more. http://swix.ch/clan/ks/CPSP1.htm

Social Psychology Glossary—text, basic, long, graphics
Provides definitions of common terms used in social psychology. Page is in alphabetical order but does not have any search or indexing capabilities. http://www.richmond.edu/~allison/glossary.html

The SocioWeb—index, interm., short, links, graphics, search
Page on sociology, a discipline closely related to social psychology, includes links to giants of sociology, sociological theory, surveys and statistics, related Web resources, and more. http://www.socioweb.com/~markbl/socioweb/

Social Cognition Paper Archive—index, interm., medium, links, graphics, search
Page contains links to paper abstracts in social cognition. Page also provides links to authors and to related resources in social cognition. http://www.psych.purdue.edu/faculty/esmith/WWW/scarch.html

News from a Social Psychological Perspective—index, basic, long, links, graphics
Links to news stories with instructive value in explaining principles of social psychology. http://miavx1.muohio.edu/~shermarc/p324news.html

Web Tutorials in Social Psychology—index, basic, short, links
Seven tutorials in social psychology including: intergroup bias in American culture, cross–cultural physical attraction, just world hypothesis, and others. http://miavx1.muohio.edu/~shermarc/p324tuta.html

Concepts and Definitions—table, basic, long
Provides definitions and results of well known experiments in social psychology: person perception, attributions, attitudes, and social influence. http://clem.mscd.edu/~psych/intro/cncpsoci.htm

VALS—index, basic, short, links, graphics
Home page of VALS (Values and Life Styles) project contains links where users can take the VALS survey, FAQ, understanding the American consumer, and other related areas. http://future.sri.com/vals/valshome.html

Gambling Practices Survey—interactive, basic, long, links
Long survey on gambling and behaviors associated with gambling. http://fremont.scs.unr.edu/~mvl/gamble.html

Web Experimental Psychology Lab—interactive, interm., medium, links, graphics
Users may take part in on–line experiments in psychology: impression formation, Muller–Lyer (requires Active X), perception (requires Java), and others. http://www.uni-tuebingen.de/uni/sii/Ulf/Lab/WebExpPsyLab.html

Counterfactual Research News—index, interm., medium, links, graphics
"How might your life have unfolded differently? What if your parents never met?" These are two questions from counterfactual psychology, a field exploring the thoughts people have about the possible unfolding of events that never happened. This site explores this area of psychology. http://www.psych.nwu.edu/psych/people/faculty/roese/research/cf/cfnews.htm

Urban Legends—index, basic, medium, links, graphics, search
Page on the urban legend, a spontaneously appearing story that contains humorous or horrific content and is usually false. Urban legends appear to have a life of their own, spreading through the culture quickly; this site categorizes and debunks them. http://urbanlegends.com

Social Psychology Chapter Quizzes—interactive, basic, short, links, graphics
Page contains 11 quizzes in social psychology with instant feedback on answers. http://www.sp.utoledo.edu/~mcaruso/social/quizzes.html

Impressions of Others

In Your Face—text, adv., long, links, graphics
Page discusses the history of research in the area of facial attractiveness, and presents original research results of an experiment. http://www.sp.uconn.edu/~marshall/html/afigure5.html

Physical Attractiveness and Face Perception—index, interm., medium, links, graphics
  Home page of a researcher in physical attractiveness, contains: on–line experiments, photos of attractive faces, related resources, and more.
  http://www.cops.uni-sb.de/ronald/home.html

Social Cognition—text, interm., long, links
  Page describes schema theory, types and actions of social schemas, and mindlessness.
  http://www.glam.ac.uk/schools/humanities/psychology/ps214/lectures/wk5.htm

Popular Culture and the Art of the Stereotype—text, adv., long
  Long outline covering the use of stereotypes in popular entertainment from the minstrel show to modern times.
  http://www.csbs.utsa.edu/users/jreynolds/popcul.txt

Ethnic Images in the Comics—index, interm., short, links, graphics
  Page contains ten articles from an exhibition of the same name about history, Jewish characters, African–American characters, Chinese characters, and more.
  http://www.libertynet.org/~balch/comics/comics.html

Superstitions Persist on Yale Campus—article, basic, medium, links
  From *Yale Daily News* (1995), provides examples of the illusory correlation at work at Yale. http://www.yale.edu/ydn/paper/3.24/3.24.95storyno.BB.html

Attributions

Attribution Theory—tutorial, basic, short, links
  Discusses several versions of attribution theory: Heider's, Jones and Davis's, and Kelley's. Also briefly comments on attributional errors.
  http://www.sci.monash.edu.au/psych/courses/1022_97/social/social5.htm

Relationships

Early Childhood–Family/Peer Relationships—index, basic, medium, links
  Page has links to full–text articles about early life relationships.
  http://ericps.ed.uiuc.edu/npin/respar/texts/fampeer.html

"Friends" Raping Friends—text, basic, long, links
  Linked page on date rape: causes of date rape, danger signals, effects, and more.
  http://www.cs.utk.edu/~bartley/acquaint/acquaintRape.html

Violence Against Women Office—index, basic, short, links, graphics
  Home page of office of the same name within the Department of Justice, contains links to information and resources about violence against women and its prevention. http://www.usdoj.gov/vawo/

Dating Practices Survey—interactive, basic, long, links
  Long questionnaire for singles on their dating practices.
  http://fremont.scs.unr.edu/~mvl/

Marriage Relationship Inventory—interactive, basic, long, links
Long questionnaire for married people on the dynamics of their marriages.
http://www.unc.edu/~schaefer/survey.htm

International Society for the Study of Personal Relationships (ISSPR)—index, adv., long, links, graphics
Home page of the ISSPR, contains links to information about the group and its journal, *Personal Relationships*. http://www.uwinnipeg.ca/~isspr/

Types of Love—tutorial, basic, long, links, graphics
Page covers types of love, the love test, sexuality standards, and much more.
http://world.topchoice.com/~psyche/love/

The Nature of Attraction and Love—text, interm., long, links, graphics
From Mental Health Net, explores attraction and love: exchange theory, infatuation, dependency, beliefs about love, and kinds of lovers.
http://www.cmhcsys.com/psyhelp/chap10/chap10c.htm

Attitudes

Behavior and Attitudes—tutorial, interm., long, links
Page covers predicting behavior from attitudes, predicting attitudes from behavior, self–presentation theory, cognitive dissonance theory, and self–perception theory.
http://www.carleton.ca/~rthibode/chapter4.html

Cognitive Dissonance—tutorial, interm., medium, links
Discusses Festinger's theory of cognitive dissonance.
http://www.gwu.edu/~tip/festinge.html

Elaboration Likelihood Model—graphic, basic, short, graphics
Page has short definition of elaboration likelihood model and chart of how the model works.
http://www.glam.ac.uk/schools/humanities/psychology/ps214/elm.htm

Conformity and Obedience

Compliance—tutorial, basic, long, links, graphics
Discusses Solomon Asch's landmark studies on compliance; includes biography, method, results, discussion, and analysis.
http://caps.otago.ac.nz:801/grant/PSYC/COMPLIANCE.HTML

Social Influence: The Science of Persuasion and Compliance—index, basic, short, links, graphics
Page contains a multitude of links on social influence and compliance, including: structure of social influence, cults, framing, and more.
http://www.public.asu.edu/~kelton/

Steve's Primer on Persuasion and Influence—index, interm., short, links
Provides 15 articles on persuasion and influence: dual–process models, attribution, consistency, reactance, modeling, and more.
http://www.as.wvu.edu/~sbb/comm221/primer.htm

Propaganda and Psychological Warfare—index, basic, long, links, graphics
Page includes sections on propaganda theory and analysis, contemporary fascist propaganda, Holocaust revisionists propaganda, political propaganda, religious propaganda, psychological warfare, and more.
http://www.lafayette.edu/mcglonem/prop.html

Cultic Studies—index, basic, short, links, graphics, search
Page provides information about cults; includes links to: Bookstore, Cult Awareness Network, *Cult Observer, Cultic Studies,* and more. http://www.csj.org/

A Teacher's Guide to the Holocaust—index, basic, short, links, graphics
Site on the Holocaust is organized as follows: timeline, people, arts, resources, activities, and credits. http://fcit.coedu.usf.edu/holocaust/

United States Holocaust Memorial Museum—index, basic, short, links, graphics
Home page of the museum of the same name in Washington D.C., page has links to information about the museum and its exhibits. http://www.ushmm.org/

Remembering the Holocaust—index, basic, long, links, graphics, Java
Page has links to 21 sites about the Holocaust: Simon Wiesenthal Centre, the Anne Frank House, Holocaust pictures exhibition, and more.
http://home.vicnet.net.au/~aragorn/holocaus.htm

The Cult Controversy—index, basic, medium, links, graphics
A look at cults over the years from the pages of the *Washington Post.* Includes stories, analysis, and debate about cults.
http://wp4.washingtonpost.com/wp-srv/national/longterm/cult/cultmain.htm

Jim Jones's Temple of Doom—article, basic, long, links, graphics
From the *Washington Post* (1988), describes the Guyana mass suicide from the viewpoint of 10 years after it occurred; includes information on the fate of survivors of the massacre.
http://wp4.washingtonpost.com/wp-srv/national/longterm/cult/people/people1.htm

The Cult That Left as It Lived—article, basic, long, links, graphics
From the *Washington Post* (1997), discusses the Heaven's Gate cult and their mass suicide.
http://wp4.washingtonpost.com/wp-srv/national/longterm/cult/heavens_gate /main.htm

Gangs in Los Angeles County—index, interm., short, links, graphics
Page has links to articles on gangs in Los Angeles: history, gang life, homicides, and more. Also has links to other Web resources on gangs.
http://www-bcf.usc.edu/~aalonso/Gangs/

Group Processes

Bystander Intervention—text, basic, short, links, graphics
Page relates the story of Kitty Genovese, a woman murdered in view of more than 30 bystanders. That incident sparked research in the bystander effect.
http://psychstan.stmarytx.edu/psysight/stuarts/stuart8-1.htm

Violence on Television—text, basic, long, links, graphics
From APA, discusses research and implications of watching violence on television.
http://www.apa.org/pubinfo/violence.html

Traffic Psychology—index, interm., long, links, graphics
Comprehensive site on the psychology of driving and traffic: origins of traffic
psychology, three domains of driving behavior, automatization of driving behavior,
and much more. http://www.soc.hawaii.edu/~leonj/leonj/leonpsy/traffic/tpintro.html

Hindering Factors in Decision Making—tutorial, basic, medium, links
Page discusses phenomena which promote poor decision making. Specific examples
are Social Loafing, Abilene Paradox, Freeriding, Groupthink, and Risky Shift.
http://chip.eng.clemson.edu/htdocs/psych499/decision/main_decision.html

Preventing Groupthink—tutorial, basic, short, links
Page offers five ways to prevent groupthink, a phenomenon blamed for faulty
decision making by highly cohesive groups.
http://www.fis.utoronto.ca/people/faculty/choo/FIS/Courses/LIS2149/PreventGT1.html

Social Facilitation—interactive, interm., short, links, graphics
From EXPERSIM, users may "run" a two–stage experiment on social facilitation
and then interpret the results.
http://samiam.colorado.edu/~mcclella/expersim/introsocial.html

How to Buy a Car—index, basic, short, links, graphics
Page has links to information and advice on how to buy new and used cars.
http://www.edmunds.com/edweb/consumer.html

Literature and Culture of the American 1950s—index, interm., long, links,
graphics, search, Java
A long alphabetized list of writings from the 1950s and links to related sites.
http://dept.english.upenn.edu/~afilreis/50s/home.html

Culture Change—tutorial, interm., short, links, graphics
Page discusses the dynamics of cultural change: processes of change, acculturation,
global change, and more. http://daphne.palomar.edu/change/default.htm

Prejudice

Intergroup Bias in American Culture—tutorial, interm., medium, links, graphics
Page covers various forms of bias found in American culture, including bias in the
political spectrum, academic spectrum, and urban spectrum.
http://miavx1.muohio.edu/~shermarc/p324bias.html

NAACP On–line—index, basic, short, links, graphics
Home page of the NAACP, a group devoted to combatting racism.
http://www.naacp.org/

National Council on Disability—index, basic, short, links, graphics
Home page of the federal agency dedicated to ensuring the rights of the disabled.
http://tiny.iapnet.com/ncd/

Anti–Defamation League (ADL) On–Line—index, basic, short, links, graphics, search
Home page of the ADL, an organization devoted to combatting anti–semitism and other forms of hatred, prejudice, and bigotry. http://www.adl.org/

Gay and Lesbian Alliance Against Defamation (GLAAD)—index, basic, medium, links, graphics
Home page of GLAAD, an organization devoted to combatting anti–gay attitudes and behaviors. http://www.glaad.org/

Just for Fun

Social Psychology Humor—index, basic, long, links, graphics
Page links to cartoons that have instructive value in explaining principles of social psychology. http://miavx1.muohio.edu/~shermarc/p324cart.html

Prisoner's Dilemma—interactive, basic, medium, links, graphics
Users may play on–line version of prisoner's dilemma game. Link on page leads to explanation of the importance of the game to theories of social psychology. http://serendip.brynmawr.edu/bb/pd.html

Rejection Lines—text, basic, short, links
Humorous listing of rejection lines used by women and men, and what they really mean. http://sputnik.ethz.ch/~miguel/humor/funnies/Rejection_lines.html

18

Research and Statistics

All psychology is based on information and techniques like those found in this chapter. The repeated efforts of instructors over the years to teach statistics, research methods, ethics, and graphing bear fruit in the publication of each new article and book. Psychology is the behavior of psychologists, and many psychologists spend their time collecting, analyzing, and reporting data. Knowing how to conduct research in psychology is an essential skill to students. The URLs below should help students hone their research skills. The URLs are grouped by the categories of: General Resources in Research and Statistics; Experiments; Mechanics of Research; Ethics of Research; Statistics; Visualizing Data; and Just for Fun.

General Resources in Research and Statistics

Statistics on the Web—index, interm., long, links, graphics
A comprehensive page on statistics on the Web includes: professional organizations, educational resources, software–oriented pages, mailing lists, discussion groups, and more. http://www.execpc.com/~helberg/statistics.html

Research Design Explained (3rd ed.)—book, basic, short, links, graphics
On–line version of text of the same name covers topics in basic statistics and research design. http://spsp.clarion.edu/mm/RDE3/start/RDE3start.html

American Statistical Association—index, interm., short, links, graphics
Home page of the American Statistical Association, provides information about the organization and links to tutorial topics to be presented at future meetings. http://www.amstat.org/

Chance Database—index, interm., medium, links, graphics
Comprehensive set of resources for teaching and learning in statistics: lectures, discussions, teaching aids, links to other Web resources, and more. http://www.geom.umn.edu/docs/snell/chance/welcome.html

Bill Trochim's Center for Social Research Methods—index, basic, short, links, graphics, search
Comprehensive site on research methods includes links to *The Knowledge Base* (a text, see below), selecting statistics, student papers, and related links. http://trochim.human.cornell.edu/

The Knowledge Base—book, basic, short, links, graphics
On–line text in research methods offers comprehensive coverage of topics in research methods with provision for users to add topics or material directly to the page. http://trochim.human.cornell.edu/kb/kbhome.htm

Statistical Measures—index, basic, medium, links, graphics
Has links to several statistics sites, definitions, and formulas.
http://www.cc.gatech.edu/classes/cs6751_97_winter/Topics/stat-meas/

Elementary Statistics Applets—index, basic, short, links, graphics, Java
Page provides Java applets that perform the following statistical tests:
student's–t, ANOVA, simple least squares, and Spearman's rank correlation. The
page also has links to help and to a basic guide to statistics.
http://intrepid.mcs.kent.edu/~blewis/stat/index.html

National Opinion Research Center—index, interm., short, links, graphics, search
Home page of the National Opinion Research Center (NORC) specializes in
"...survey research in the public interest." Provides links to a general social survey,
overview and history, publications, and more.
http://www.norc.uchicago.edu/homepage.htm

Globally Accessible Statistical Procedures (GASP)—index, interm., short, links,
graphics, Java
Page contains a collection of on–line statistical routines (many require Java) that
users may use. Routines include: kernel density estimation, procedures for
multivariate analysis, regression applet, central limit theorem applet, and more.
http://www.stat.sc.edu/rsrch/gasp/

WebStat—interactive, adv., long, links, graphics, Java
The beta version of a new statistics package that runs on–line. Users may input
data or work from two available datasets. Requires Java.
http://www.stat.sc.edu/~west/webstat/

Statistical Education Through Problem Solving (STEPS)—download, adv.,
short, links, graphics
Site provides freely available software for statistics (Mac and PC).
http://www.stats.gla.ac.uk/steps/

Statistics Glossary—index, basic, short, links, graphics
On–line glossary from STEPS (see immediately above), provides information on
terms in the following categories: basic definitions, presenting data, sampling,
probability, random variables and probability distributions, confidence intervals,
hypothesis testing, paired data, correlation and regression, design of experiments
and ANOVA, categorical data, nonparametric methods, and time series data.
http://www.stats.gla.ac.uk/steps/glossary/index.html

PROPHET StatGuide Glossary—text, basic, long, links
Comprehensive on–line linked glossary of statistics; provides information on
statistical terms and tests. http://www-prophet.bbn.com/statguide/sg_glos.html

Statistics to Use—index, adv., short, links
Page contains information about statistical tests and links to pages that calculate
statistics for those tests: mean and standard deviation, student's t–tests,
chi–square distribution test, contingency tables, Fisher exact test, ANOVA,
ordinary least squares (with and without plotting), and more.
http://www.physics.csbsju.edu/stats/

Research Methods—index, interm., medium, links
This page lists a large number of other sites relevant to research methods including characterization of quack theories, SAS Institute, random number generators, and much more. http://cavern.uark.edu/comminfo/www/methods.html

Princeton Survey Research Center—index, interm., short, links, graphics
Home page of center contains links to polls and survey findings and data, research practice, other survey research centers, market research, and more. http://www.princeton.edu/~abelson/index.html

Junk Science—index, interm., medium, links, graphics, search
Home page of the The Advancement of Sound Science Coalition (TASSC), a group dedicated to debunking "junk science", or bad science. Page contains articles, archives, FAQs, cartoons, and more. http://www.junkscience.com/

Statistical Instruction Internet Palette (SIIP)—index, basic, short, links, graphics
Page features information and tools for teaching and learning about statistics: data gallery, equation gallery, graphic studio, computing studio, and more. http://seamonkey.ed.asu.edu/~behrens/siip/

Statistics and Statistical Graphics Resources—index, interm., long, links
Comprehensive site on statistics contains links to: statistical associations, departments, data visualization, on–line courses, statistical packages, and more. http://www.math.yorku.ca/SCS/StatResource.html

Experiments

Critical Thinking in Psychology—tutorial, basic, long, links
Teaches users about issues in the design of studies, the following topics are covered: asking testable questions, correlational vs. experimental designs, and identifying variables and confounds. Includes references for each section. http://gateway1.gmcc.ab.ca/~digdonn/psych104/think.htm

Psychological Research on the Net—index, basic, medium, links
A page where users can participate as subjects in on–line experiments and studies. http://psych.hanover.edu/APS/exponnet.html

The Number Game—interactive, basic, short, links, graphics
Users can participate in another short on–line experiment and see the data thus far. http://weber.u.washington.edu/~jlks/pick.cgi

Sexual Behavior Survey—interactive, basic, short, links
Users may participate in a survey in which some questions pertain to sexual behaviors. Limited to participants over 18 years of age. http://psych.fullerton.edu/throck/

Mechanics of Research

APA Style Electronic Formats—tutorial, basic, long, links, graphics
Page provides advice on how to cite Web and other electronic sources properly. http://www.westwords.com/GUFFEY/apa.html

Citing Electronic Resources—table, basic, medium, links, graphics
Tables list examples of various types of electronic citation: individual works, journals, magazines, and e–mail.
http://www.wilpaterson.edu/wpcpages/library/citing.htm

How to Cite Information From the World Wide Web—text, basic, short
From APA, page provides four examples for citations from the Web.
http://www.apa.org/journals/webref.html

Publication Manual FAQ—FAQ, basic, medium, links, search
From APA, this FAQ answers eight basic questions about how to write manuscripts in APA style. http://www.apa.org/journals/faq.html

Library Research in Psychology—text, basic, medium, links, graphics
Page provides hints on where and how to conduct library research in psychology. Suggests strategies for both non–psychologists and student researchers.
http://www.apa.org/science/lib.html

Ethics of Research

Ethical Principles of Psychologists and Code of Conduct—index, basic, long, links
From APA, the full text of the *Ethical Principles of Psychologists and Code of Conduct* are provided in linked fashion. http://www.apa.org/ethics/code.html

On Being a Scientist—book, interm., short, links
Full text of a book with same title published by the National Academy of Science (NAS). Topics include the social foundations of science, experimental techniques and the treatment of data, values in science, authorship practices, misconduct in science, and more. http://www.nap.edu/readingroom/books/obas/

To Harm or Not to Harm—text, basic, medium, links
On–line version of a pamphlet from the Humane Society discusses the ethics of using animals in experimentation and teaching suggests alternatives.
http://www.hsus.org/harm.html

Human Subjects/Participants and Research Ethics—index, basic, short, links, graphics, search
Covers the ethics of research: position papers and policies, courses, ethics committees, and related links.
http://www.psych.bangor.ac.uk/deptpsych/Ethics/HumanResearch.html

Statistics

G*Power—download, interm., medium, links, graphics
Users may download software that performs basic statistics and power analysis. Downloads available for Mac and PC formats.
http://www.psychologie.uni-trier.de:8000/projects/gpower.html

Descriptive Statistics Calculator—interactive, basic, short
Page calculates the mean and standard deviation for N data points.
http://www.physics.csbsju.edu/stats/cstats_NROW_form.html

Guide to Available Mathematical Software—index, interm., short, links, graphics, search

From the National Institute of Standards and Technology (NIST), this site catalogs statistical software by the problem it solves, package name, module name, and by text in module abstracts. http://math.nist.gov/

MacStats Home Page—index, interm., short, links

Page lists software packages available on the Web for the Macintosh platform in the following categories: structural equation modeling, regression/ANOVA, time series analysis, general–purpose mathematical software that can be used for statistical analysis, programs for graphing and data visualization, freeware packages for statistical analysis, bibliography of software reviews published in computer magazines, and links to other resources on the World Wide Web related to Macintosh statistics. http://www.gsm.uci.edu/~joelwest/MacStats/

***HyperStat Online* (Rice)**—book, basic, short, links, graphics

Comprehensive look at basic statistics: describing univariate data, describing bivariate data, introduction to probability, normal distribution, sampling distributions, point estimation, confidence intervals, the logic of hypothesis testing, testing hypotheses with standard errors, power, introduction to between–subjects ANOVA, factorial between–subjects ANOVA, within–subjects ANOVA, prediction, chi square, distribution–free tests, and measuring effect size. http://www.ruf.rice.edu/~lane/hyperstat/contents.html

Statistical Calculators—interactive, basic, medium, links, graphics

Page contains links to several on–line statistical calculators including power, correlation and regression, random numbers, and more. Some require additional software on client side. http://www.stat.ucla.edu/calculators/

Introductory Statistics—book, interm., short, links, graphics

Comprehensive book on statistics and their use: comparing frequency distributions, the summation sign, score transformations, normal curve areas, ANOVA, and much more. http://www.psychstat.smsu.edu/introbook/sbk00.htm

Statistical Simulations and Demonstrations—interactive, interm., short, links, graphics, Java

Page provides links to six demonstrations of topics in basic statistics: sampling distribution, normal approximation of binomial distribution (2), small effect size, regression by eye, and components of r. http://www.ruf.rice.edu/~lane/stat_sim/index.html

Normal Distribution Applets—interactive, basic, short, links, graphics, Java

Users may interact with Java applets to calculate probability and quantiles of Z scores they enter. http://playfair.stanford.edu/~naras/jsm/FindProbability.html

Random Number Generator Software Catalog—index, adv., short, links

Page has links to sites where users can obtain different types of random number generators. http://nhse.npac.syr.edu:8015/nhse-rw/catalog/random/

Introduction to Using Random Number Generators—text, interm., short, links
> By author of page above, explains how random number generators work.
> http://nhse.npac.syr.edu/random/overview.html

Critical Values of the *t* distribution—table, basic, medium, links, graphics
> Page provides the critical values of the student's t–test for the .05 and .01 levels
> for df values from 1 to 120. http://shazam.econ.ubc.ca/intro/critval.htm

Degree of Freedom—text, basic, short, links, graphics
> From Principia Cybernetica Web, a short definition of the concept of degree of
> freedom. http://pespmc1.vub.ac.be/ASC/DEGREE_FREED.html

Web Chi Square Calculator—interactive, basic, short, links, graphics
> Calculates chi squares for values users enter, gives short or long output.
> http://www.georgetown.edu/cball/webtools/web_chi.html

Chi Square Tutorial—tutorial, interm., long, links, graphics
> Teaches about the chi square test: overview, bivariate tabular analysis,
> generalizing from samples to populations, chi square requirements, collapsing
> values, computing chi square, interpreting the chi square value, and measures of
> association. http://www.georgetown.edu/cball/webtools/web_chi_tut.html

Chi Square Probabilities—Text, basic, medium
> Table of chi square critical values with dfs from 1 to 100 and p values from 0.995
> to 0.005. http://www.richland.cc.il.us/james/lecture/m170/tbl-chi.html

On–line Software for Clustering—index, adv., long, links
> Page is a cut–and–paste collection of statistics software collected from the Web.
> http://astro.u-strasbg.fr/~fmurtagh/mda-sw/online-sw.html

Visualizing Data

Summary of Tufte Seminar on Data Visualization—text, interm., long, links,
graphics
> Notes from a presentation by Edward Tufte, author of books on visualizing and
> graphing data. Summarizes some principles of good design in the presentation of
> graphical information. http://www.irf.org/irtufte.html

Minard's Map—graphic, basic, short, links, graphics
> Tufte's example of an early classic of visualization, Minard's map of Napoleon's
> disastrous Russian campaign in 1812, is shown and explained.
> http://almond.srv.cs.cmu.edu/afs/cs/project/sage/mosaic/IntelligentInterfacesLab
> /IIL.2.html

Just for Fun

Gallery of Statistics Jokes—text, basic, long, links, graphics, Shockwave
> Page consists of 32 jokes about statistics and statisticians. Shockwave is only
> required to see an animation at top of page.
> http://www.ilstu.edu/~gcramsey/Gallery.html

Random Number Generator—interactive, basic, short, links, graphics, Java
Generates six random numbers, each between 1 and 49, just like many lotteries.
http://arnie.pec.brocku.ca/~wmontelp/hfiles/649lab3.htm

Alphabetical List of Sites

Alphabetical List of Sites

B

C

Alphabetical List of Sites

Alphabetical List of Sites

Alphabetical List of Sites

Alphabetical List of Sites

IMPORTANT

**If the CD-ROM packaging has been opened, the purchaser cannot return the book for a refund!
The CD-ROM is subject to this agreement!**

Licensing and Warranty Agreement

For Technical Support:
Voice: 1-800-423-0563
Fax: 1-606-647-5045
E-mail: support@kdc.com